STEFAN COLLINI

What Are Universities For?

D1332692

PENGUIN BOOKS

PENGUIN BOOKS

Published by the Penguin Group
Penguin Books Ltd, 80 Strand, London WC2R 0RL, England
Penguin Group (USA) Inc., 375 Hudson Street, New York, New York 10014, USA
Penguin Group (Canada), 90 Eglinton Avenue East, Suite 700, Toronto, Ontario, Canada M4P 2Y3
(a division of Pearson Penguin Canada Inc.)
Penguin Ireland, 25 St Stephen's Green, Dublin 2, Ireland (a division of Penguin Books Ltd)
Penguin Group (Australia), 250 Camberwell Road,
Camberwell, Victoria 3124, Australia (a division of Pearson Australia Group Pty Ltd)
Penguin Books India Pvt Ltd, 11 Community Centre,
Panchsheel Park, New Delhi – 110 017, India
Penguin Group (NZ), 67 Apollo Drive, Rosedale, Auckland 0632, New Zealand
(a division of Pearson New Zealand Ltd)
Penguin Books (South Africa) (Pty) Ltd, 24 Sturdee Avenue,
Rosebank, Johannesburg 2196, South Africa

Penguin Books Ltd, Registered Offices: 80 Strand, London WC2R 0RL, England

www.penguin.com

First published 2012
003

Copyright © Stefan Collini, 2012
All rights reserved

The moral right of the author has been asserted

Set in 9.25/12.5pt Linotype Sabon
Typeset by Jouve (UK), Milton Keynes
Printed in Great Britain by Clays Ltd, St Ives plc

ISBN: 978-1-846-14482-0

www.greenpenguin.co.uk

MIX
Paper from
responsible sources
FSC™ C018179
www.fsc.org

Penguin Books is committed to a sustainable
future for our business, our readers and our planet.
This book is made from Forest Stewardship
Council™ certified paper.

ALWAYS LEARNING   **PEARSON**

To my colleagues and students,
who have taught me what universities are for

Contents

Introduction

Asking what something is *for* all too often turns out to be asking for trouble. There is, to begin with, the danger of seeming to reduce a complex activity or institution to a single, narrow purpose: it is doubtful whether an answer that is both short and illuminating could be given to questions about what, say, love is *for* or a country is *for* – we immediately sense that any answer is bound to be a tiresome mixture of banality and tendentiousness. And then there is the problem that any answer may seem to invite the same question – 'Yes, but what is *that* for?' – spiralling down into an endless regress. As the ball of reasoning starts to roll down the slope of justification, we realize that our likely destination is a muddy pond of abstract nouns in which all distinctiveness gets lost. But any intermediate stopping-point is bound to seem arbitrary and, for that reason, vulnerable to somebody giving the ball another nudge. This situation recalls that old cartoon which depicted a truculent and precocious small child, head in hands on the kitchen table, saying to an exasperated parent standing nearby: 'I was merely observing that "Because is why" seemed to me to contain a hidden premise.' History does not record whether the child went on to become a distinguished philosopher (or, indeed, survived into adulthood at all).

But, sometimes, asking what something is 'for' can, if understood as an expository tactic, a starting-point rather than a ruling, be a means of helping us to clear away the discursive debris that accumulates round any widely used category. The very asking of the question in this slightly over-insistent, finger-jabbing form may be enough to encourage reflection to cut through the incidental clutter and begin to wonder what kind of response could count as a useful answer. From then on, it is probably sensible not to try to press the question further in this narrow form, but to let rumination extend itself, brooding on the diversity that may shelter under a single term, pondering a series of characterizations or historical instances rather than seeking a single defining proposition. That, certainly, will be the tactic of this book. But the initial question will already have done its work if it helps to launch such a train of reflection, thereby giving us some distance from the numbingly familiar repetition of a few stock phrases in news stories and comment columns. John Maynard Keynes famously asked 'What is economics for?', using that question to remind his readers that the pursuit of wealth was not an end in itself but a means to living 'wisely, agreeably, and well'. Keynes's example is pertinent, and inspiring, because any discussion of the place of universities in contemporary society will inevitably be driven to articulate, in however rudimentary terms, some sense of human purposes beyond that of accumulating wealth.

Or so one might think. Yet it is scarcely an exaggeration to say that the greater part of public discourse about universities at present reduces to the following dispiriting proposition: universities need to justify getting more money and the way to do this is by showing that they help to make more money. This book is an attempt to start from somewhere else and to talk about universities in a different way.

Since there is an obvious risk that my arguments in this vein will be misinterpreted and misrepresented in some quarters (I still bear some bruises from earlier attempts to make this case), let me say emphatically here that I – and, I believe, pretty much everyone else who works in or cares about universities – do not for a moment underestimate the expense of these institutions or presume that there is some God-given right for them to be lavishly funded. Of course the case for their value and importance needs to be made. But it needs to be made in appropriate terms, and these terms are not chiefly, and certainly not exclusively, economic. They are intellectual, educational, scientific, and cultural. In addition, it has to be emphasized that higher education is a public good, not simply a set of private benefits for those who happen to participate in it, and therefore that it is a mistake to allow the case for universities to be represented as a merely sectional or self-interested cause on the part of current students and academics.

This book argues that we shall not identify the distinctive character of universities if we concentrate on the ramifications of one or another local, and necessarily temporary, model of funding them. Similarly, we shall not come very close to understanding the true character and interest of intellectual enquiry if we start from the presuppositions of those who believe that such enquiry is a luxury whose economic benefit remains to be demonstrated. And nor will we arrive at an adequate grasp of what is, or should be, involved in a university education, as opposed to various other forms of instruction and training, if we start from the current preoccupation with 'access'. 'Funding', 'impact', 'access': these three starting-points – taken either singly or, more often, as a trinity signalling the realism and up-to-dateness of one's position – now utterly dominate the political and media discussion of universities in Britain. But these are secondary matters, and the last two, in particular, are merely transient formulae – clumsy articulations of aspects of social attitudes to which politicians find it expedient to appeal. When I take issue with these fashions, as I do in Part Two, my focus is on the assumptions underlying them, not (except incidentally) on recommending some alternative set of arrangements.

In Part One, the main part of the book, I begin by offering a sketch of the place of universities in modern societies, followed in the second chapter by a short account of the history that lies behind the current situation in the UK. In Chapter 3 I explore, initially by way of a dialogue with John Henry Newman's classic text, *The Idea of a University*, the relations between the ideal of a 'liberal education' and the goal of extending human understanding. Taking that argument further, Chapter 4 goes on to focus particularly on the nature and role of the humanities – not, needless to say, because I believe they are more central to a university than the natural and social sciences, but partly because their character and value are usually less well understood than that of the scientific disciplines, and partly simply because they are the disciplines with which I am most familiar. Then in the fifth chapter I undertake a more frankly polemical engagement with what are at present the dominant characterizations of the functions of universities. In Part Two I follow a different strategy by offering several examples of the way in which criticism of official policy towards universities in recent years can provide the opportunity for infiltrating into public discourse a more adequate characterization of their nature and purposes. The chapters in Part Two are on the whole briefer, more satirical, and more opportunistic; they are attempts to bring some of the larger considerations outlined in Part One to bear on current debates in a pointed and topical way. These chapters also bear witness, in a necessarily episodic form, to the sharply accelerating way in which successive governments, of whichever party, have attempted to impose an increasingly economistic agenda on universities over the past two decades.

Since what I have to say about universities is partly a reflection on practice, I should indicate at the outset the kind of practice of which I have most direct experience. In the broadest terms, my own writing and teaching have been in the overlapping fields of literature and history. More particularly, my work has been concerned with aspects of the literary and intellectual culture of (largely) Britain in the nineteenth and twentieth (and now twenty-first) centuries, including the history of its universities. What I have to say would no doubt be different if my own background were in, say, philosophy or music or classics or art history, and perhaps more different still if it were in one of the social or natural sciences. I should also acknowledge that the experience on which I am drawing has been gained from working in comparatively favourable circumstances within highly regarded and (for the most part) well-supported universities, first at the University of Sussex from the mid-1970s to the mid-1980s, and subsequently at the University of Cambridge. I recognize that anyone who works in such institutions needs to be regularly reminded that the activities of teaching and scholarship may have to be pursued in much more constraining circumstances elsewhere.

Although I believe that many of the issues I address in this book are common to universities in several countries, and although I hope that my contentions may resonate with those facing similar problems in other places, I make no apology for the fact that I derive my themes and my illustrations principally from my experience of British universities, and that I likewise couch my arguments in terms that seek to engage with the condition of public debate on this topic in contemporary Britain. For the most part, I must leave those with more knowledge of universities and public debate in other countries to decide how far what I say applies to the cases they are familiar with. The responses from elsewhere in the world to essays I have written over the years about aspects of the British situation encourage me to think that it is not too difficult to find illuminating parallels.

What Are Universities For? is not a philosophical monograph any more than it is a White Paper. The literary category to which it most nearly approximates may be that of the polemic, which in turn overlaps with the genres of satire, jeremiad, manifesto, and essay in cultural criticism. The contract with the reader which such genres offer is founded on the notion of persuasiveness. They do not attempt to compel assent by means of either logical indefeasibility or empirical comprehensiveness, and they do not rest their case on thoroughly worked-out proposals. They aspire instead to bring the reader to focus on and recognize something hitherto neglected, misdescribed, undervalued, or suppressed. And the process of recognition is always in part an appeal to something which the reader, at some level, already knows – otherwise, what is being described could not be genuinely recognized; it could only be registered. I hope that all kinds of readers will find this book informative as well as persuasive, but above all I hope readers will *recognize* in these pages a case that speaks to their half-buried intuitions about what universities are for, and that it thereby encourages and assists those readers to make this case tell in the public domain.

PART ONE

I
The Global Multiversity?

I

Universities across the world in the early twenty-first century find themselves in a paradoxical position. Never before in human history have they been so numerous or so important, yet never before have they suffered from such a disabling lack of confidence and loss of identity. They receive more public money than they have ever done and yet they are more defensive about their public standing than they have ever been. At a moment when the number of students currently enrolled in these institutions across the globe is several times larger than was the case only a generation ago, there is unprecedented scepticism about the benefits (both intellectual and material) of a university education. While in some quarters universities are heralded as engines of technological advance and economic prosperity – and developing nations rush to establish more of them in pursuit of these goals – elsewhere they are attacked for being 'self-indulgent', 'backward-looking', and 'elitist'.

These tensions take various forms depending on local circumstance and cultural tradition, but the sheer scale of university expansion around the world in recent decades indicates that much is expected of these curious institutions – perhaps too much, or at least perhaps not exactly what they are best designed to provide. Societies which hope their newly founded universities will become powerhouses of economic development tend to strike a more upbeat note when discussing them than do those richer Western societies whose long-established institutions fear that the instrumental discourse of

3

modern market democracies is becoming impatient with the traditions of open-ended enquiry which have hitherto been these institutions' distinguishing feature. Within universities, those in technological, medical, and professional disciplines are generally more confident that the future belongs to them than their colleagues in the humanities or even many branches of the 'pure' sciences. A professor of accounting and business studies in Singapore or a professor of metallurgy in Wuhan may understandably feel that universities have never been so popular or so well-resourced. A professor of medieval history in Ohio or a professor of German literature in Sheffield may feel that their disciplines, and their careers, have never been so precarious or so little esteemed.

Because the huge expansion of recent decades has involved a growth not just in student numbers but also in range of subjects and types of institution, it is too late in the day to attempt to be insistently purist about the usage of the term 'university': for better or worse it is now applied to a great variety of forms of post-secondary educational institution. These institutions serve several important social functions, from vocational training to technology transfer, just as they further several admirable social goals, from inculcating civic values to enabling social mobility. Nothing I say in this book is intended to disparage those functions and those goals, or to deny that they now play an important and legitimate part in the life of several types of higher education institution in many countries. But those are clearly not the distinctive or defining features of universities, and in asking what universities are 'for', one is obviously inviting reflection on their character at a rather different level. I am not here positing an ideal university, nor am I suggesting (as will become very clear) that 'proper universities' used to exist but have now been diluted or distorted out of all recognition. Instead, I am asking how we should now understand and characterize what is distinctive about what universities do, what differentiates them from (while still sharing some characteristics with) schools, research laboratories, learned associations, museums, and so on.

It is an interesting feature of the historical story that the label or concept of 'university' has acquired a prestige and a potency such that, in some countries, attempts are made to affix it to institutions that have practically nothing in common with those European and North American universities of the nineteenth and twentieth centuries that earned this prestige in the first place. In such cases it is sometimes just used to designate an institute of post-secondary-school training. But even in making that observation, am I, implicitly, making a contrast with a type of institution which does more than, or at least other than, that? And if so, why does that other type of institution have any better claim to the label? One answer is that it may have a better claim simply because it seems nearer to the type of institution which originally acquired this prestige. After all, existing universities have rarely if ever tried to appropriate the name and the character of technical institutes, teacher-training colleges, agricultural schools, and so on: the flow of emulation has always been in the other direction. So in such cases we need to consider what characteristics of 'the university', apart from the prestige, are being laid claim to.

Not only do universities operate within different cultural and (to some extent) intellectual traditions, but their relations to their respective states vary enormously, especially their financial relations. A well-endowed private university in the United States may indirectly get a substantial part of its income from Federal funds through research grants and special programmes, but at bottom it is an independent corporation free to set its own goals and raise its own revenue. A middling state university in the same country can find its future almost wholly determined by fluctuations of local opinion as expressed in the state legislature. Practically all British universities are overwhelmingly reliant on public funding, but while these monies have increasingly come with some tightly drawn strings attached, successive governments have (so far) respected the principle of the autonomy of universities, as laid down in their charters, largely leaving them to determine their own internal affairs, including their academic programmes. In many parts of continental Europe, universities, which may be legally obliged to admit any student with the relevant school-leaving qualification, are directly under the control of the national or regional minister for education. Such institutions are seen as direct instruments of government policy, including various forms of social assimilation and the inculcation of civic values, while elite education and research is often heavily concentrated in a small number of 'grandes écoles' and state-run research institutes. In some parts of Asia, the Middle East, and Latin America, universities which are in effect wholly state-run technical colleges, specializing in subjects such as engineering and agriculture, sit alongside wholly private institutions, often specializing in economics and business studies, which depend largely on the fees from children of relatively wealthy families. In our larger meditations on this topic, we tend to speak freely of 'the university', as though all these various types of institution partook of some common informing ideal or essence, but it is not easy, faced with this bewildering array, to see what this might be.

The task is made more difficult still by the great multiplication of subjects of study and research. In reality, many universities have long offered courses that went beyond the traditional core of disciplines in the humanities and natural sciences, but there has been a marked expansion of such courses in recent decades. Diplomas in golf-course management sit alongside MScs in software design; professorships of neo-natal care are established alongside postdoctoral fellowships in heritage studies. In addition, universities are increasingly centres of the creative and performing arts as well as hubs of policy advice, while those in countries influenced by the Anglo-Saxon tradition may also be major nurseries of athletic achievement. 'Multiversity' was the term introduced, perhaps only half-seriously, in 1963 by the then Chancellor of the California university system, Clark Kerr, to capture the huge variety of activities now carried on in a major research university. As a label, it has not really caught on, but I use it at several points in this book to signal a recognition of that plurality.

For some purposes, it would be right to take a cue from the plural form of my overall title and to say that since the label 'university' has been applied to so many kinds of institution we should not look for anything like a single answer. But I suspect that, to most readers, this would look like a bad case of ducking the question. Still, what is it for a characterization of universities to be adequate to their (extremely diverse) existing reality? Obviously, we are looking for something more than mere statistical or taxonomic summary, something which captures their quiddity as institutions, the distinctiveness of teaching or studying in them, by contrast to a range of other social institutions.

II

As an absolute minimum, the modern university might be said to possess at least the following four characteristics:

1. That it provides some form of post-secondary-school education, where 'education' signals something more than professional training.
2. That it furthers some form of advanced scholarship or research whose character is not wholly dictated by the need to solve immediate practical problems.
3. That these activities are pursued in more than just one single discipline or very tightly defined cluster of disciplines.
4. That it enjoys some form of institutional autonomy as far as its intellectual activities are concerned.

This is obviously a pretty spare characterization, but it may already start to suggest why the form has seemed desirable. The structure of all four features depends on an implicit contrast with something more restricted, something that lacks the hard-to-specify yet alluring range and freedom of the characteristic in question. At the same time, even this minimal initial inventory begins to suggest why these institutions may be so problematic for their host societies. It seems as though they are bound, by their nature, to be constantly going beyond whatever particular menu of tasks society may set for them. The very open-endedness of their principal activities threatens to legitimate forms of enquiry that may run counter to the aims of those who founded or supported them. One begins to wonder whether societies do not make a kind of Faustian pact when they set up universities: they ask them to serve various purposes, but if they are to be given the intellectual freedom necessary to serve those purposes properly, they will always tend to exceed or subvert those purposes. Representatives of the 'lay' public – or, in the more statist regimes, government officials – may be installed on ruling councils and other superintending bodies, but they cannot effectively regulate all that goes on in the libraries and laboratories. Societies want the scholars and scientists in their universities to extend understanding and discover new knowledge, but those activities have their own logic which cannot be gainsaid without a risk of jeopardizing the enquiries themselves. Of course, in some cases extreme measures can be taken to prevent research and writing departing too far from the official script: for example, a few professors can be shot *pour encourager les autres*. But in broadly liberal societies such measures are frowned on, and subtler means have to be found to manage the inevitable tensions between prevailing definitions of social purpose and the ungovernable play of the enquiring mind.

In addition to these four minimal features, universities (at least those which, in the main disciplines, have PhD programmes or the equivalent) have a further peculiar characteristic that can make it hard for other forces in society to exert a satisfactory level of control over them. Universities are among the very few institutions whose rationale includes selecting and shaping their own future staff. Schools educate everyone: it is not a distinctive part of their remit to form and prepare future school-teachers. Companies recruit new staff and train them in the appropriate techniques, but this is a secondary task, not part of their primary rationale, which is to produce goods or services and make a profit. By contrast, the forming of future scholars and scientists is not just an instrumental necessity for universities, but intrinsic to their character. Educating someone to pursue the open-ended search for deeper understanding has to be a kind of preparation for autonomy. This makes it unusually difficult for those outside universities to specify how this professional preparation should be carried out, and so the academic profession – by its very nature rather than as a pathological form of self-interest – will be bound to appear self-absorbed as well as self-recruiting in a way in which most other social organizations will not.

Since universities are in some ways puzzling and opaque institutions, attempts to describe them naturally tend to bracket them with more familiar or immediately intelligible concepts. Perhaps the most frequent, because most plausible, misconception about universities is

8

that they are simply a marriage of convenience between a type of school and a type of research laboratory. There are, of course, continuities with these two institutions, but it is the discontinuities that are more fundamental and more interesting. One neat, but therefore only partly adequate, formulation says that while schoolchildren are taught, university students study. Undergraduates are being introduced to the modes of enquiry appropriate to various disciplines; what they develop, ideally, is not simply mastery of a body of information, but the capacity to challenge or extend the received understanding of a particular topic. For this reason, university teaching has more than its share of the paradox involved in *telling* someone to 'be autonomous!' Learning what is involved in conducting enquiry in a certain discipline partly grows out of being exposed to examples of such work and then being incited, not to reproduce them, but to produce a piece of work of one's own that is informed by having come to understand what the examples are examples *of*. This can only be done by becoming acquainted with work in a particular discipline: simply being exhorted in general to pursue truth, cultivate accuracy, express oneself clearly, and so on, will not achieve the desired goal, though being encouraged to subject those abstract expressions themselves to analytical scrutiny might conceivably be the beginnings of an education in philosophy.

Research laboratories of a kind maintained by some big corporations or by certain charities, especially those which support medical research, bear a close resemblance to one aspect of life in university science departments, and there is a good deal of trade between the two types of institution in terms of ideas and personnel. But here the main differences are of setting and scope, though differences in ethos can sometimes also be revealing. Research labs not based in universities tend to have goals which are fairly strictly circumscribed by the character of their parent organization. It is true that a large corporation will encourage its most highly qualified research staff not just to refine and improve its current products but to push against the boundaries of the present state of the field in ways which may generate new ideas and, eventually, new products. And in some industries, such as information technology or aerospace, some of the most fundamental work may be done in these labs by scientists who might be equally at home (if less well funded) in a university computing or engineering department. Nonetheless, there are limits to the range of work which a corporation's R&D team can undertake, and such focused research programmes are always partly parasitic on the more open-ended enquiries pursued in universities. Although such research labs may sometimes train staff in particular techniques, and may even occasionally have doctoral students or postdoctoral fellows temporarily working alongside company staff, they do not educate undergraduates or confer doctorates, and they are by and large dependent on universities for the supply of highly qualified scientists. Microsoft or Boeing or BP or other large corporations in highly technical industries may help to advance knowledge in certain fields, but they do not function like universities, nor would their shareholders look kindly on any attempt to do so.

Analogies between universities and quite other types of institution may, precisely because they are less fashionable, be more illuminating. Some, at least, of what lies at the heart of a university is closer to the nature of a museum or gallery than is usually allowed or than most of today's spokespersons for universities would be comfortable with. The latter would doubtless be afraid that it would make universities seem too conservative or complacent, too 'backward-looking' – a damning phrase from the lexicon of contemporary right-mindedness, though we might, on reflection, have to acknowledge that most of what we reflect on and try to understand is necessarily in the past. A facile contrast can be made between the research laboratory and the museum in respect of their relation to time, where the former is seen as oriented to the future and to discovery while the latter is concerned with the past and with preservation. But this familiar contrast obscures not just the ways in which a museum expresses a constantly changing relation to human understanding and is the home of all kinds of advances in knowledge, but, more importantly, the ways in which any scientific community is embedded in, indeed partly constituted by, the practices and observations of its predecessors. Moreover, neither of these institutions exists in a vacuum: they require a very extensive cultural infrastructure, including not only the long-drawn-out education needed for curators and conservers and researchers, but the wider world of scholarship and science which sustains them. One of the reasons why the question: 'What are museums/galleries for?' can be helpful in thinking about universities is precisely because it reminds us that the answers do not depend just on the interests of the current generation. All conservation, all transmission or handing-on, and in fact all enquiry, is implicitly governed by its relation to the future.

Neil MacGregor, the Director of the British Museum, recently observed that the purpose of such an institution is that of 'giving people their place in things'. Applauding this sentiment, the historian David Wootton added that the purpose of the discipline of history is 'to give the past its place in us'. At one level, these self-consciously epigrammatic remarks do not take us very far, but perhaps, at another level, they do point to something that museums and universities have in common, something to do with enabling individuals to place them-selves in relation to the world, and especially to time. This is certainly not confined to the humanities: finding one's 'place in things' could just as appropriately be said of enquiries in physics and astronomy or in psychology and anthropology as it could of those in history or literature or philosophy.

The partial parallel between universities and museums can be exploited to make another important point in relation to current debates. In the provision of a whole range of what are called 'cultural attractions', as in the provision of most types of education, great emphasis is now laid on making the subject-matter 'accessible' to the relevant publics, on making sure that they are not deterred by finding it alien or difficult. But this emphasis always needs to be balanced by a parallel insistence on the interest of what is strange or initially hard to comprehend. This is not an argument for deliberate obscurity or forbiddingness, but a recognition of the fact that for many people the sheer otherness of an object (or an idea) may be the source of its fas-cination. The mind is engaged much more fully by trying to understand something that initially resists our categories than by encountering a further instance of what is already familiar. Just as a museum can lose much of its power over the imagination if its collection is confined to items it is assumed people will easily 'relate to', so a university course can forfeit much of its disconcerting and mind-stretching effect if it takes too narrow a view of what is 'relevant' or 'attractive'. Where enlarging the understanding is concerned – either the understanding of an individual at a particular point in their maturation, or the understanding of a society at a particular point of its history – we have to make space for the difficult and the alien and not underrate the educative power, on the imagination as well as the intellect, of the brute unresponsive residues of space and time.

There are other aspects of universities that may suggest resemblances to a variety of quite different types of organization – to think-tanks, performing arts complexes, and apprenticeship programmes, as well as to sports clubs, community centres, and dating agencies. In addition, as we are now often reminded, universities are large employers and one of the chief sources of prosperity for local economies. But all of these comparisons pick up on what are contingent or inessential features of universities, on functions which have come to be appended to their main tasks of extending understanding through teaching and research. It has often been remarked how, in some of the larger American universities with proud sporting traditions, the football coach is more highly paid than the university's president. It is well understood how this is bound up with those universities' dependence on the support and generosity of alumni and donors and the part that is played by sporting success in sustaining this particular kind of local patriotism. Viewed from a different cultural perspective, it is hard not to see this as yet another pathology of systemic commercialism, but in any event no one, I assume, would be likely to claim that football, or any other sport, is centrally what universities are 'for' or what defines their distinctive character. And the same can be said of those other contingent or inessential features of universities that current metaphors and analogies emphasize: their distinctiveness does not lie in their being large employers or generators of spin-off companies or concentrations of policy advice, any more than it does in their being centres of early-career sporting prowess or providers of cheap beer. The contemporary multiversity, as that tag suggests, houses a vast array of activities, but that does not mean that we cannot still distinguish between the core functions of universities and, on the one hand, the various secondary activities which have clustered round them, or, on the other, those social and economic effects which are by-products or indirect consequences of their main purpose.

III

But is that main purpose really sustainable when the world, including the world of higher education, is changing so fast? Sooner or later some form of this question obtrudes itself: consciousness of an accelerated pace of social and economic change appears to be one of the defining characteristics of contemporary reflection. In reality, something similar seems to have been no less true of earlier generations; they, too, thought that the speed of change had quickened in their own time and that in consequence old verities were called into question. Nonetheless, the question has, initially, to be addressed in its own terms. If we are asking what universities are 'for', must we not recognize that their nature and purpose has been radically changed by globalization? Shouldn't we stop thinking in terms of the nineteenth-century European ideal and focus instead on how it is the Asian incarnation of the Americanized version of the European model, with schools of technology, medicine, and management to the fore, which most powerfully instantiates the idea of the university in the twenty-first century?

The fashion for slapping the adjective 'global' in front of a wide variety of nouns often simply indicates a mixture of slackness and hype. The word has come to be treated as a more dramatic-sounding synonym for 'international'. But perhaps it can still be rescued and made to do an honest day's work. There is some point to describing a pattern or development as 'global' when the trans-national similarities being identified are both sufficiently widespread and the result of common causes, especially causes that stem from economic development. Since scholarship and science are inherently supranational activities, there have always been instances of universities in one country learning from or imitating those in another, and from the late

nineteenth century onwards the existence of European empires naturally led to the transplanting of domestic models to other parts of the
world. But what may have been relatively new in the last couple of
decades of the twentieth century, and even more marked in the past
ten years, is the simultaneous transformation of the scale of higher
education in almost all 'developed' (and some 'developing') countries,
along with the concomitant introduction of similar organizational
and financial arrangements which cut across, and have sometimes
signalled major departures from, existing national traditions.

A recent comparative study summarized the main features of
change by drawing up two lists (inevitably presented as bullet-points)
which contrasted the forces generally at work in higher education
systems in the mid-twentieth century and those at work today. Not all
the points listed may seem equally important or equally well framed,
but the overall direction of the contrast is surely right and is instructive.

The first list, headed 'Major forces influencing higher education
50 years ago', reads as follows:

- Initial era for building mass higher education systems
- Higher education seen largely as a public good
- Limited adoption of international higher education models
  and practices – higher education as an extension of national
  culture
- National and regional markets for undergraduate students
  and institutional prestige
- High institutional autonomy – limited accountability
  measures
- Government as partner with the higher education community
- National accreditation and quality review
- Traditional pedagogy – limited technological adoption
- Substantial government subsidization
- Small for-profit sector – mostly in US
- Beginnings of a burgeoning scientific community
- Limits on cross-national knowledge sharing and
  communications

The second list is entitled 'The new globalization', offering point-for-point comparisons:

- Maturing era for mass higher education systems in most developed nations
- Higher education increasingly viewed as a private good
- Growing international adoption and convergence of higher education practices and models – higher education as an extension of globalization
- Growing international and supranational market for undergraduate students and institutional prestige
- Eroding institutional autonomy – growing accountability measures
- Government as adversary with the higher education community
- Possible international accreditation and quality review
- Changing pedagogy – growing technological adoption
- Declining government subsidization – rising student fees, growing diversity of funding sources/privatization
- Growing for-profit sector
- Established scientific community
- Global knowledge sharing and communications

One quick and easy recipe for cultural criticism – one frequently used by columnists in the more conservative newspapers to whip up their weekly soufflés – is to arraign today's developments by yesterday's standards, and clearly there is a risk for anyone writing about universities of taking the features in the first of these lists as providing the benchmark of virtue against which those in the second list may be judged as failings. But not only would that indicate a rather unintelligent form of conservatism, and one doomed to irrelevance: it would also fail to attend to the heterogeneity of the features that are being compared. For example, it is hard to see how the use of 'technology' in teaching could be seen as anything other than a neutral adoption of the inventions available in the wider society: the replacement of quills by fountain-pens, or the replacement of handwriting by type-writing, was no more or less the loss of something integral to the purposes of universities than has been the replacement of typewriting by word-processing (which is not to say that the new capacities of current information technology do not mark a transformative change in both teaching and research). In a different vein, one might also wonder whether it is really accurate to see only the 'beginnings of a burgeoning scientific community' fifty years ago, with 'an established scientific community' as a new and recent development: communication has certainly speeded up, and the worldwide use of English has facilitated this, but the change here, such as it is, really looks like only the intensification of a pattern that had been at work for much longer, and certainly cannot be represented as a falling-away from some truer or purer standard. By contrast, the question of whether higher education is thought of as a 'public' rather than a 'private' good may seem to involve much larger convictions about how societies function as well as being likely to entail a more straightforwardly evaluative response.

But at the heart of both lists is a cluster of features that obviously signals a change in the scope of the relevant communities of reference, with the national more and more being supplanted by the international. One obvious aspect of this is increased mobility of students: the United States and Britain were for some time the most favoured destinations, but in more recent years other countries, such as Singapore or Australia, have operated as major regional recruiters. In the late 1990s Australian universities were directed to increase their income from overseas students, with the result that such visitors soon came to compose over 25% of the student body, but in recent years even this percentage has been comfortably exceeded by some individual universities in Britain, the USA, and elsewhere, especially at postgraduate level (the London School of Economics has particularly focused on attracting international postgraduates, so that by 2010 60% of its total student body were said to be from overseas). Less obvious, perhaps, at least to Anglophone readers, are schemes such as the 'Bologna accord' in Europe, which attempts to install a uniform cycle of first degrees, masters, and doctorates across countries which had previously adhered to widely differing classifications and timetables. Part of the rationale for such schemes is to facilitate movement between national systems; in some cases, semester-long 'modules' have also been imposed as the teaching pattern with the same intent. But perhaps the most conspicuous, if also most egregious, sign of this heightened concern with international comparisons is to be found in the obsession with global 'league tables' of universities. Where their supposed findings are convenient, these are readily cited for publicity and propaganda purposes, yet the truth is that they are practically worthless. On many matters the data are not available in strictly comparable form, and the use of subjective and inadequate opinion surveys, such as the 'student satisfaction' survey, provides little information that is both reliable and useful. Moreover, these league tables (there are several now in operation, with the 'Shanghai world rankings' generally receiving greatest attention) give disproportionate weight to 'big science': the resulting rankings tell us something about the level of expenditure on research projects in the sciences in the various universities, and that is allowed to stand as a proxy for the more intractable problems involved in deciding whether one university is, in any sense that could matter, 'better' than another.

The significance attributed to these largely vacuous exercises indicates the conjunction of two forces which bear directly on the discussion of the role of universities. The first is the glib assumption that universities are locked in combat with each other in some form of worldwide competition, itself a transposition of larger assertions about the centrality of national economic competitiveness. The language here betrays a kind of mercantilism of the intellect, a fear that the stock of national treasure will be diminished rather than augmented by the success of enterprises elsewhere. It is remarkable how quickly and easily this language has become naturalized in the past two or three decades, even though it is damaging to the intrinsically cooperative nature of all science and scholarship. The second force is the growing distrust of reasoned argument, now often seen as either a cloak for special interests or a form of elitist arrogance, and the substitution in its place of any kind of indicator that can plausibly be reduced to numerical terms. The latter possess the aura of both precision and objectivity and so, when joined with the assumption about competition, can generate a definitive ranking. Vice-chancellors now keep as nervous an eye on league tables as do football managers, and placings are frequently invoked to legitimate a preferred policy shift.

In this way, discussion of universities, as of many other matters, has become afflicted with 'Champions League syndrome'. It is assumed that all the 'top' universities 'play' in the same 'league' – I deliberately make the quotation marks intrusive to call attention to the misleadingness of these familiar metaphors. National amour propre, ever a vain and giddy quality, comes to be invested in having universities that might give the big American powerhouses a good game. Once again, the results are principally measured in terms of research in the biological, physical, and medical sciences, and those results are in turn largely determined by financial investment. Many of the ways in which an institution might be a good university and play an important part in the intellectual life of its host society are simply disregarded. In Britain, the discussion mostly reduces to whether Oxford and Cambridge and Imperial College are 'competing' with Harvard and Stanford and MIT; in certain other countries attention is focused on getting one or more universities in the world's 'top 50' or 'top 100'. The question of whether, say, the Norwegian or Swiss higher education systems serve the needs of their respective populations well is not asked (I choose the examples at random, not on account of particular features of those systems), and there is, anyway, no means of translating the answers to such questions into the pseudo-objectivity of tabular form. The transnational character of intellectual enquiry long pre-dated fashionable talk of 'globalization', just as the ways in which it is inherently collaborative give the lie to the cant about international 'competition'. Both 'global' and 'multiversity' are, in short, terms which need to be treated with some caution, not to say scepticism (an injunction which may be unnecessary in the case of the latter and ineffective, though very necessary, in the case of the former).

One way to point to the significance of recent changes would be to say that life in universities is now *less unlike* life in other large organizations than at any time in the long history of these singular institutions. Traditionally, attempts to characterize what universities were for would have been likely to invoke the great cultural icons of intellectual enquiry, from Plato in the Athenian Academy onwards, perhaps in the twentieth century celebrating those Nobel laureates and prize-garlanded scholars whose achievements were assumed to have arisen out of a cloistered form of life, insulated from many of the world's pressures. But the distracted, numbers-swamped, audit-crazed, grant-chasing life of most contemporary academic departments is as far removed from classical ideals of the contemplative life as it is from what was until recently supposed to be the form of existence represented by the metonomy of 'the senior common-room'. The experience of being a senior academic now, especially one involved in chairing a department or directing a research centre, may seem to more closely resemble that of being a middle-rank executive in a business organization than it does that of being an independent scholar or freelance teacher, while the conditions of work of junior and temporary staff in some unfavoured institutions may, in the limiting cases, suggest comparisons with those of staff in a call centre. Any tract such as this one has, on pain of irrelevance if not derision, to acknowledge and address these changed circumstances. But in doing so, it has to try not simply to repeat the shibboleths and catchphrases which these circumstances have brought in their train. The aim of this book is, while being realistic and reasonably well-informed about the contemporary state of universities, to start from further away in order to revitalize ways of understanding the nature and importance of universities that are in danger of being lost sight of in the present.

2
Universities in Britain:
A Very Short History

I

Every politician is a closet historian, and so is every armchair critic. It is not just that all analyses of 'what needs to be done' about higher education rest, as do discussions of almost any policy, upon assumptions about the way the world is moving, but, more specifically, that every position taken about universities rests on unexamined claims about what universities 'used to be like'. Universities have been around a long time – and so have many of the participants in these discussions. There is an understandable tendency for the latter to think that universities must always have been pretty much what they half-remember them being in their day. Such patchy, impressionistic history can then be made to support either of the two almost equally unappealing extremes around which opinion tends to congregate. On the one hand there is the mournful idiom of cultural declinism: 'standards' are falling, 'philistinism' is rampant, 'autonomy' has been lost, and even the barbarians are going to the dogs. And on the other, there is the upbeat idiom of brave new worldism: 'challenges' and 'opportunities' abound, 'partnerships with industry' beckon, 'accountability' rules, and we're all 'investing in the future' like billy-oh. As with larger questions of social and cultural change, it can be difficult to escape the magnetic pull of these extremes, difficult to get the measure of the changes that have been taking place without falling into the absurdity of suggesting that everything would be all right if we could just go back to universities as we think they were c. 1959, or the equal absurdity of proposing that more ruthless cost-cutting and more aggressive marketing could soon have HiEdBizUK plc showing healthy profits for shareholders.

Attempts have been made, principally among those more sympathetic to the first rather than the second of these extremes, to arrive at a defining statement of the 'idea' of the university, a timeless essence, a yardstick against which contemporary developments can be measured and found wanting. These attempts have generated some fruitful reflection and critique, but they are too often vitiated by a conservative or nostalgic desire to 'restore' some version of the university that pre-dates the era of mass higher education. Many of these embattled declarations seem to hope that the ritual invocation of Newman's *The Idea of a University* will ward off the most threatening features of contemporary conditions (I explore a different way of entering into dialogue with this Victorian classic in the next chapter). Hardly surprisingly, no deathless prose has been written on 'The Idea of a Tertiary Education Sector'. The truth is that the different justifications currently offered for universities are a series of residues from earlier stages of social and educational development. Over and over again, as Sheldon Rothblatt, one of the foremost historians of British universities, pointed out some years ago, we meet attempts to define an ideal of university education 'by joining principles and values that at bottom have different historical origins and acutely different cultural meanings and purposes'.

This is certainly the case with the numerous ahistorical pronouncements one currently encounters about what defines a 'real' university or about what a 'proper' university education ought to be, and so forth. On closer inspection, these pre-emptive definitions usually turn out to rest on a few selectively recalled details about the way certain British universities functioned in the 1950s and 1960s, abstracted from the conditions which sustained them. Similarly, in current discussions about university funding, and especially about student support, it is often assumed that the system now undergoing such radical overhaul has been in place time out of mind. In fact, it was only at some point in the decade after 1945 that the state started to provide even half of the income of any British university, and it was only after the report of the Anderson Committee in 1960 that a national system of mandatory grants for students was put in place. Since then, the pace of change has been so fast that no decade can plausibly be chosen to represent the 'normal' condition of the system. It is worth remembering that when the Thatcher government's *Kulturkampf* against universities began in 1981, nearly half of Britain's forty-six degree-granting institutions had not been in existence as universities two decades earlier. From one point of view, the 1980s and 1990s look like the decades during which successive governments attempted to reduce the 'historic' standing of universities and dismantle their 'traditional' funding structure; but, taking another historical perspective, it is the 1960s and 1970s that can be made to appear exceptional, the first and last decades in which Britain tried to sustain a substantial but still rigorously selective, wholly state-funded system of high-quality, undergraduate-centred universities. The fact that almost two thirds of the degree-granting institutions operating in the UK in 2011 did not even exist (at least as universities) as recently as twenty years ago only underlines the importance of not treating the situation thought to obtain at a given moment as any kind of timeless norm.

II

It is tempting, partly in order just to tease those who complain that current practices in universities are 'positively medieval', to suggest that no sensible thinking about universities can be done without going back to their origins in the Middle Ages. Certainly, the general prospectus for a recent large-scale publishing venture entitled 'A History of the University in Europe' makes a striking claim to this effect: 'The university is the only European institution to have preserved its fundamental patterns and basic social role and function over the course of the last millennium.' Striking – but is it true? There is a remarkable apparent continuity in terms of form: a largely self-governing community of scholars, organized around several intellectual disciplines, teaching advanced students. I say 'apparent' because of the obvious distance separating this model from the current version of highly managerial corporate enterprises in which scholars are rather lowly employees. But perhaps the continuity in 'role and function' is no less questionable. The juridical entities that were established at Bologna in (perhaps) 1088, in Paris and Oxford around (probably) the middle of the twelfth century, and in Cambridge in (arguably) 1209, were overwhelmingly ecclesiastical institutions, though in time they acquired some importance as centres of secular study and teaching in fields such as law and philosophy. This ecclesiastical character predominated all over Europe until at least the era of the French Revolution. These institutions chiefly trained future functionaries of state and church, or provided a kind of finishing school for the landed elite. For the most part, the advances in scholarship and science that started to transform the intellectual world of early-modern Europe did not happen in universities, but either in separate institutes and academies, or in independent associations of learned gentlemen. Part of the fascination of the history of universities is the way in which the traditional model has adapted to such developments, and has absorbed or supplanted potential rival types of institution. In several European countries today, a small number of 'academies' survive, sometimes largely as learned bodies, essentially honour-societies for senior scholars, occasionally as free-standing centres of scholarship and research. However, 'the university' has, without question, become the dominant form.

But although universities do have this long history, there is no need, for present purposes, to dwell on these more distant periods. For the truth is that the modern university is essentially a nineteenth-century creation. The establishment of the University of Berlin in 1810 by Wilhelm von Humboldt, then the Prussian minister for education, is conventionally regarded as a symbolic founding moment, and certainly for the next half-century or so German scholarship and science, as conducted in the newly vigorous universities inspired by Humboldt's ideal, set the standards by which provision and achievement elsewhere were measured. Universities came to be seen not simply as the nurseries of future clerical or administrative functionaries, but as centres of 'the higher learning'. Research was coming to be seen as part of the defining purpose of the university, both in the expanding fields of the natural sciences but also, and perhaps even mainly at this date, in those fields that were later to be designated as the humanities and social sciences, especially in history, philosophy, philology, and the study of classical literature. The elaboration of the modern system of academic ranks accompanied this enhanced sense of the value of scholarly achievement, expressed in the division between 'the professor' of a certain subject and his 'assistants' (later called 'lecturers' in the British model), with some form of career progression from the latter title to the former. The systematic education of the next generation of scholars became part of the programme of universities, with various kinds of doctorate or higher degrees being awarded. In the later part of the nineteenth century, young scholars from Britain and the United States flocked to Germany to benefit from such training, and soon (in the 1870s and 1880s in the USA, slightly later in Britain) PhD programmes were being established in the larger universities in these countries as well as elsewhere.

Although different national systems of higher education each have their own distinctive characteristics, scholarship and science are inherently international enterprises and so no one system can be understood wholly in isolation from the others. By the later nineteenth century, the dominance of the German universities was at its peak. They were hugely influential in the United States, both intellectually and organizationally, and they constituted a source of rivalrous curiosity in France, especially after the defeat of 1871, but they had considerable impact in Britain, too, not least in standing for an ideal of *wissenschaftlich* 'research', which came to be grafted onto the native traditions of teaching and scholarship. However, although much of the initial intellectual inspiration for the growth of European universities had come from Germany, by the twentieth century it was the major British and American universities that increasingly provided not just the dominant models for emulation elsewhere but also the nearest approximation to the Humboldtian ideal of combining a liberal education with advanced scholarly and scientific research. The British Empire led directly to the establishment of universities around the world modelled on the 'home' institutions, in practice more along the lines of London or the Scottish or larger civic universities than of Oxford and Cambridge, though this latter pair continued to exert a gravitational pull when it came to postgraduate work and visiting fellowships. In higher education as in so much else, French territories overseas tended to be treated as part of the metropolitan system, and thus the French model left its mark in parts of Francophone Africa and elsewhere after independence. Similarly, there were resemblances between universities in Latin America and the Iberian template, albeit that the dominant intellectual traditions in this case often came from Germany. But the fact is that the vast expansion and re-shaping of universities across the world in the later decades of the twentieth century rarely, if ever, involved emulation of contemporary French or German or other continental European systems; the balance of trade has all been in the opposite direction, with the 'Anglo-Saxon' model setting the pace throughout the world, Europe included. Many of the proposals (and some of the policies) of recent years have been explicitly aimed at trying to make universities elsewhere, notably in Britain, more closely resemble their American counterparts, or at least some imagined version of them. Quite what form the Chinese university is taking, and will in turn export elsewhere as that country rises to economic dominance in the course of the twenty-first century, remains to be seen, but at present it certainly looks like a local adaptation of the Anglo-Saxon model.

From the outset, the German ideal embodied tensions which have, in one form or other, continued to mark universities to this day. Humboldt's university itself was a curious mixture of *Lehrfreiheit* and state control, a cross between a self-governing community of scholars and a collection of civil servants. In addition, there was the long-standing tension between serving a variety of social needs and being in some way withdrawn from society, even offering a form of resistance to the dominant values and practices of that society. Universities had always been practical, providing the church with its personnel or staffing state bureaucracies, and yet always also pursuing studies that did not bear directly on any of those tasks. In earlier centuries, the study of law and medicine had been classic cases of useful subjects which generated fields of scientific enquiry of their own. Something similar could be said about subjects as diverse as engineering or Oriental languages in the middle and later decades of the nineteenth century. Increasingly, universities were involved in what has been termed the 'credentializing' process, a mechanism for assuring society that only those with approved qualifications will be allowed to practise a particular profession. And the very success of universities in taking over the training of future professionals and embedding it in an environment of 'the higher learning' meant that all kinds of practical concerns turned to the university as a source of, simultaneously, validated qualifications, the benefits of the latest research, and cultural prestige and respectability. Agriculture provides a less obvious example of a subject-matter which was initially introduced into universities entirely for practical reasons, as in the 'land-grant' colleges of the USA in the later nineteenth century, but which then helped sustain the expansion of those institutions in directions that were far less immediately practical. Some of these developments can be seen in another way as a tension between, on the one hand, the claims of the 'host' society and its needs, and, on the other, the pull exerted by transnational ideals of science and scholarship. The activities of academics in Berlin or Paris or Oxford or Stanford came to be determined at least as much by what was being done by colleagues in the same discipline in other countries as by any immediate civic or social priorities, a state of affairs with which governments and other local sponsors have often been uneasy. Geographical mobility on the part of university teachers and students has expressed and reinforced this sense of belonging to an intellectual community which transcends national borders.

So, through all this expansion of scope and function, a fundamental tension remained discernible in the rationale of universities, as it still does today. Put most simply, the imperative to pursue the fuller understanding of any subject-matter once it was established as part of an academic discipline constantly tended to exceed and subvert the imperative to meet immediate or local needs. Chairs could be established in, say, Law in order to train future lawyers, but the enquiries some of these professors then pursued led them to fundamental questions about the nature of authority or the history of different social ideals or the acceptable limits to free expression, and many similar topics. Professors of law were constantly turning into legal historians and legal philosophers and even social theorists more broadly (much of the nineteenth century's thinking about the evolution of types of society was conducted by those appointed to teach law). These sub-disciplines then became accepted parts of the syllabus, and the whole subject became over time more recognizably 'academic' – a tricky, loaded word, but one which here suggests the pull away from the practical to forms of enquiry with their own protocols and ambitions. The same drift is very evident in the history of the science faculties so often established with the hope of benefiting local industry through inventions and other technological advances, but in time passing over into what is now often called 'blue-skies research', enquiries driven by the intellectual logic of the discipline rather than by the imperative to address an immediate practical problem. And here we touch on one of the great strengths of the university and one of the keys to its remarkable longevity: while serving other needs, it also simultane-ously provides a supportive setting for the human mind's restless pursuit of fuller understanding. Perhaps it is hardly surprising that so many hopes and aspirations have come to be invested in this peculiar institution.

III

At the time of the French Revolution, there were seven universities in the British Isles: two in England (Oxford, Cambridge), four in Scot-land (Edinburgh, Glasgow, St Andrews, Aberdeen), and one in Ireland (Trinity College, Dublin). For the most part, they enjoyed greater autonomy from the state than the French and German models at this date, though they tended to be more closely identified with the relevant established churches than their continental counterparts. In the earlier decades of the nineteenth century, it was the venerable Scottish universities which made the liveliest intellectual contribu-tions, drawing on indigenous democratic traditions and a strong emphasis on professional studies such as law and medicine. In Eng-land in the 1820s and 1830s, two new colleges were founded in London (University College and King's College), and a tiny Anglican outpost established at Durham, but otherwise the sleepy monopoly of Oxford and Cambridge was not seriously challenged. It was in the mid- and late-Victorian period that two developments took place that were to determine university development in Britain for almost a hundred years. First, the colleges of Oxford and Cambridge, which had long functioned as a cross between agreeable clubs for the sons of the landed classes and seminaries for the Anglican church, were reformed. The public-school ideal of character-formation took hold; 'modern' subjects, such as history, natural science, and modern languages, were introduced; a new self-consciousness developed about educating the governing and administrative class of the future; and the sense of the universities' place in the national culture grew. Secondly, in the 1870s and 1880s new institutions were established in the great cities which had grown up as a result of industrialization, such as Birmingham, Manchester, Leeds, Sheffield, and Liverpool. Initially, these colleges were the result of local initiatives and were aimed at meeting local needs: they were not afraid to teach practical subjects such as 'commerce' alongside the traditional curriculum; many of their students lived at home; some of the students were women. A different 'idea' of the university was required to take account of these institutions. The device of the 'royal charter', recognizing and legitimating their standing but also guaranteeing them a degree of autonomy, has survived as the main legal mechanism by which the state simultaneously controls and liberates the universities.

Thus, by the beginning of the twentieth century there were already at least three different kinds of institution among British universities, quite leaving aside the various medical schools, teacher training colleges, and numerous ecclesiastical, voluntary, and professional institutions. There was the Oxbridge model: residential, tutorial, character-forming. There was the Scottish/London model: metropolitan, professorial, meritocratic. And there was the 'civic' model ('Redbrick' was a later coinage): local, practical, aspirational.

From the early years of the twentieth century a dialectic was already at work which was to become one of the dominant forces in the development of higher education in Britain, a dialectic that was at least partly powered by snobbery: the newer and different types of institution increasingly shed their distinctiveness and more and more conformed to the culturally dominant model. Thus, the civic universities progressively lost their local and practical character: they built more and more residences for students from other parts of the country; the traditional hierarchy of subjects reasserted itself; playing fields came to be regarded as essential to a university education, a historically curious association that still looks quaintly Anglo-Saxon when viewed from Berlin or Paris. And this is a pattern which has since been repeated with other relative newcomers: first, in the 1940s and 1950s, with the former local colleges that granted external London degrees (such as Hull, Leicester, Nottingham, Reading, Southampton); then in the 1960s and 1970s with the Colleges of Advanced Technology (such as Bradford, Brunel, Loughborough, Salford, Surrey); and then again in the 1980s and 1990s with the polytechnics. The pull has always been towards being a national rather than a local institution; towards offering a full spectrum of subjects; towards offering postgraduate as well as undergraduate degrees; towards supporting research as well as teaching; and towards having the autonomy and prestige traditionally associated with (though in recent years fast being lost by) the older universities.

Even so, universities expanded slowly in the first few decades of the twentieth century in Britain; on the eve of the Second World War, fewer than 2% of the population passed through them; they were not, for the most part, objects of media attention; and many of the recently founded civic institutions were very small and somewhat fragile. Moreover, the state had played hardly any direct role in financing universities until after the First World War; they were either autonomous foundations with their own endowments, or the result of local initiative and funding, or dependent on students' fees (or, usually, some combination of these). Only in 1919 was a body established to distribute the small grant-in-aid which governments had begun to make to some institutions. Called the University Grants Committee, this was essentially an arrangement for protecting the autonomy of universities by allowing a small group mostly made up of senior academics to act as an intermediary body to advise the government on the needs of universities and then to distribute such sums as the Treasury should allocate for the purpose. These were not large: in the 1930s the annual recurrent grant for all universities in Britain only amounted to about £2 million. But after 1945 the pace of growth quickened, and, of course, as the state increasingly came to provide the finance it increasingly asserted its will. In re-shaping the landscape of higher education in recent decades, three main forces have been at work, and not just in Britain, though the process has taken a distinctive form here. The first is the explosion in student numbers; the second is the vast expansion of scientific research; and the third is political ideology.

The statistics showing the growth in numbers are eloquent enough. In 1939 there were about 50,000 students at the twenty-one university-level institutions in Britain (all such figures are disputable; even now matters of definition dog the attempt to produce agreed statistics). Post-war expansion saw this figure more than double to 113,000 by 1961. Thereafter, the rate of expansion accelerated sharply. Many people, including those who hold forth about universities, still think that the new 'plate-glass' universities of the 1960s (Sussex, York, Essex, East Anglia, Warwick, Kent, Lancaster) were set up as the outcome of the famous 'Robbins Report' (the report of a committee on the future of universities chaired by Lionel Robbins), but simple chronology indicates how far from the truth this is. It was at the end of the 1950s that the UGC took the initial decision to found new universities, and the first of them, Sussex, opened its doors in 1961; the Robbins Committee did not report until 1963. It also has to be remembered that although several of these new universities introduced (in the words of Sussex's manifesto) 'a new map of learning' – that is to say, they tried various means of getting away from the single-honours, department-based degree – the institutions themselves were conceived along very traditional lines. They were fairly small and highly selective in their intake; they were residential, built on green-field sites just outside attractive English regional towns (rather than in the bigger urban centres); they placed a strong emphasis on the traditional idea of close pedagogic and social contact between students and teachers (some even had 'colleges' on the Oxbridge model); and they were primarily committed to a 'liberal education' in the arts and sciences. This familiar identity was, if anything, confirmed when, two years after the Robbins Report, Anthony Crosland, the then Secretary of State for Education, enunciated what became known as 'the binary principle', according to which two different but parallel types of higher education were to be developed: the traditional kind in universities and a more vocationally oriented, community-responsive kind in the polytechnics.

It is also sometimes forgotten that, as far as the number of institutions was concerned, the situation arrived at by the late 1960s remained unchanged for a couple of decades or more. No new universities were founded between 1969 and 1992 (apart from the anyway exceptional case of the New University of Ulster). But student numbers were rising fast: by 1980 there were around 300,000 students in forty-six universities, with ever-higher targets being set for each year's intake. However, in 1992 the re-classification of the former polytechnics almost doubled the number of universities overnight (38 former polytechnics eventually gained university status), and since 2000 more than thirty other institutions, usually former higher education colleges, have also gained their university charter. All these institutions have, especially in the past decade, been under relentless political and financial pressure to take more and more students, with the result that the total has been driven up to over two and a quarter million – studying at (depending, as always, on one's classification) some 130 university-level institutions. These totals mask particularly striking increases in the numbers of postgraduate students and those studying part-time at whatever level; in the last three decades the number of postgraduates has gone from around 60,000 to over 530,000, while part-time students, rare at university level in the past, now account for over 855,000 of the total. These figures also mask the gigantic educational enfranchisement of women that has taken place in the course of the last fifty years to the point where female students are now slightly in the majority. Almost inevitably, staff–student ratios have declined in the past three decades (from an all-time high of 1:8 to more than 1:22 according to some calculations, though such average figures mask wide variations), resulting in many cases in an alarming reduction in the number of 'contact hours' and amount of personal attention each student receives.

During the same period, universities have been transformed to the point where many are now principally centres of scientific and technological research and, increasingly, of vocational and professional training. In the 1930s, half the students at British universities were in the arts faculties; more strikingly still, at Oxford and Cambridge the proportion studying in arts faculties were 80% and 70% respectively. In 2009, those studying pure 'humanities' subjects (classification problems again) accounted only for some 11% of undergraduates and 9% of postgraduates in British universities, though a wider classification of 'arts, humanities, and social sciences' would yield a much higher proportion. The percentages studying the 'pure' sciences have risen significantly since the 1930s, but the really huge gains have been registered in the past couple of decades by vocational and 'applied' subjects. A few illustrative figures may help bring home the scale of the change. The two most popular arts subjects are still, as they have long been, English and history: in 2009, 60,000 were studying the former and 52,000 the latter (undergraduates and postgraduates combined). In the same year, 131,000 were doing law, 148,000 engineering, 293,000 'subjects allied to medicine' (which excludes those doing medical degrees, a further 63,000), and, the all-time chart-topper, 330,000 doing business studies and accountancy. We have, to put it mildly, moved a long way from Newman's idea of a university, and public debate about higher education can often seem under-informed about the extent of the recent transformation.

Alongside these developments, there have been quite remarkable changes in the scale and objects of expenditure by universities, above all expenditure on research rather than teaching. The huge growth in the costs of 'big science' and the extraordinary expansion of the scope of the biological sciences, in particular, mean that the science budget has now soared into the billions, dwarfing the amounts spent on the humanities and social sciences (for example, the combined budgets of the seven research councils in the UK amount to some £3 billion, but only around 3% of this goes to the Arts and Humanities Research Council). Public funding of higher education is now heavily concentrated on supporting science, medicine, and technology, and these departments account for an overwhelmingly large proportion of any individual university's operating budget. It is hardly surprising that so many of the characteristics of the funding system under which universities now operate, from the reliance on winning large grants from commercial and charitable sponsors to the categories of the Research Assessment Exercises, should reflect the economic clout of the sciences.

These first two sets of changes have been cumulative, only partly deliberate, and often barely noticed as they were taking place. But the impact of political ideology, especially when viewed from within universities, has been dramatic, programmatic, and controversial. Up until the late 1970s, universities expanded on the back of what might be called the 'welfare-state model of cultural diffusion'. As with the arts, the traditional form of some cultural good was to be extended to more and more people by means of state support. 'Culture' was seen as an antidote to or refuge from the grubby pressures of economic life, and universities were expected to be beacons of culture. This model had its paternalist side – the mandarins knew what was worth having more of, whether people clamoured for it or not – and also its hidden subsidies to the middle class, who were overwhelmingly the chief beneficiaries of the expansion before the 1990s. But it also had deep roots in British social attitudes, and although the shocks sustained by the British economy in the course of the 1960s and 1970s entailed periodic re-jigging of university funding, they left the assumptions governing this model more or less intact.

Thereafter, four dates marked successive stages of a calculated assault by Tory governments on institutions which they perceived as expensive, self-absorbed, arrogant, and subversive. In 1981 a savage reduction in university funding was implemented, in a move that appeared almost deliberately to undermine rational planning and damage morale. Across the whole system, the reduction was of the order of 11%, in some places it was much higher – several universities, including one or two of the most highly regarded, suffered sudden funding cuts of around 20%, and the University of Salford (one of the former Colleges of Advanced Technology so smiled upon in the Harold Wilson/C. P. Snow years) saw its budget cut by over 40%. The second key date was 1986, which saw the first of the Research Assessment Exercises, the brainchild of the then Chairman of the UGC, Sir Peter Swinnerton-Dyer. This was an attempt to measure the quality of the research carried on in different departments; the resulting ranking would determine the amount of the 'research' element in the block grant going to any given university. This was a key step towards the all-devouring audit culture that has since so signally contributed to making universities less efficient places in which to think and teach. The third date was 1988, the year of the 'Great Education Act' which, among other things, changed the legal status of academic tenure and abolished the UGC, putting in its place funding bodies empowered to give direct effect to successive government policies largely by making funds dependent upon compliance in carrying out various reforms or in meeting specific targets. And the fourth was 1992, when legislation enabling the former polytechnics to become universities came into force, thereby ensuring that policies for the now much larger university sector would be based on lower-cost models of 'mass' education less deferential to the status that had previously accrued from exclusiveness or historic association. (For example, by 2009 eighteen of the twenty-five largest universities in the UK in terms of student numbers were former polytechnics, geared to meeting needs rather different from those catered to by traditional universities.) By and large, the universities, even the most prestigious of them, offered remarkably little resistance to these changes, bending the knee whenever their funding masters passed by.

In the 1980s and early 1990s the Thatcher and Major governments expanded student numbers without providing corresponding investment in universities, deliberately driving down the 'unit cost' of higher education. They also attempted to impose a particular conception of 'efficiency', which entailed changes in governance to make universities more closely resemble the business-school conception of a well-run commercial company (although in the business world itself the wisdom of strictly top-down, Chief Executive models has increasingly been questioned). So, in the long march that has seen universities function as seminaries, finishing schools, government staff colleges, depositories of culture, nurseries of citizenship, and centres of scientific research, they were now to turn themselves into plcs. After 1997, the Blair governments tried to mitigate the effects of long-term underfunding, though new money was often for strictly earmarked purposes and tied to continuing 'reform' (for the introduction of 'top-up' fees, see Chapters 8 and 10 below). But the overall direction of change remained constant.

Faced with these developments, it is no good simply saying that universities are autonomous bodies and what goes on inside them is none of the state's business. That idea would have seemed pretty odd at most times and places in the history of universities, whether in Renaissance England or eighteenth-century Germany or, for that matter, modern France. It is true that Britain has had a long tradition of leaving various functions to be performed by independent, local, and voluntary bodies, which then become suspicious of or resistant to state 'intervention'. But even the colleges of Oxford and Cambridge, prime examples of this style of legally autonomous corporation, were investigated and eventually reformed by successive Royal Commissions in the middle and late nineteenth century; they were forced to make proper use of endowments and to direct the education they offered towards what were seen at the time as national needs (particularly for the training of an administrative class). And wherever the state has become the piper, tunes have been called. The UGC served as a useful buffer, deferring the full consequences of this logic until the later decades of the twentieth century, but it has long been apparent that universities cannot have it both ways: if they want reasonably generous financial support from the government of the day, then they have to accept becoming answerable to that government and its conception of what the electorate will bear. On this score, the two most frequently reiterated goals of official policy have for some time been, first, to make universities more responsive to the needs of the economy, and, second, to expand numbers and achieve a 'truly democratic inclusiveness' while simultaneously promoting 'social mobility'.

As many observers have pointed out, arrangements and assumptions that may have worked well enough when around 6% of the age cohort went to university (the proportion in the mid-1960s) are simply bound to be put under strain when 45% are doing so. Fifty years ago universities benefitted from a more general cultural deference, and notions of an education suitable for those who were to occupy 'leading positions' in society still had some purchase. Diluted versions of some of the customs of the social elite could still seem integral to a university

35

education rather than contingent historical trappings. The dramatic transformation of Britain and comparable societies in the later decades of the twentieth century, especially increased prosperity and greater egalitarianism, have called many of these assumptions about university education into question. The three-year, post-18, residential, single-subject, exam-assessed, arts or science course is no longer the only model and may soon be very far from the dominant form of tertiary education in this country. As I have already indicated, the majority of students at a large number of British universities now study vocational or professional subjects, many of them on a part-time basis, many of them as 'mature students'. Moreover, most of the largest universities (in terms of student numbers) are not what is now called 'research-intensive' institutions; they have evolved from former polytechnics or higher education colleges with a different remit and a different culture. (One of the minor benefits that might come from public discussion catching up with the reality of the scale of the present higher education system in Britain would be an end to, or at least a diminution of, the obsession with Oxford and Cambridge in certain parts of the media.)

In the wake of this history of dramatic expansion, one of the challenges facing the British higher education system in the early twenty-first century is to decide how far all the institutions called 'universities' should attempt to provide the same range and level of activities. Analogies with systems in other countries are dangerous, and anyway we have to start from where we are, but one of the more intriguing, and most discussed, foreign models was Clark Kerr's (largely realized) plan for three major tiers of higher education in California – ascending from local community colleges to the large-enrolment California State Universities and above them the campuses of the University of California (including Berkeley and UCLA). One of the features of this system, as of American higher education more generally, is that it caters for student mobility between types of institution and thus allows opportunities for second (and third ...) chances – something Britain has, historically, been bad at providing. The California system was intended to be socially inclusive in terms of opportunity but frankly hierarchical in terms of intellectual ambition. There are, of course, problems, and nothing maps perfectly from one system onto another, but this example provides some pointers towards the shape of a higher education structure that has managed to be both enlightened and diversified, just as it has more recently provided a dire warning of the vulnerability of publicly funded systems to the changing moods of the electorate and its political representatives.

Still, some such diversification may lie ahead for universities in Britain. It may not make sense for them all to be offering, say, doctoral qualifications in all or most of the traditional academic subjects any more than it makes sense for all of them to have hugely expensive medical or engineering schools or for all of them to offer diplomas in various ancillary roles within the social services. It may be desirable for some universities to be selective in the range of subjects they offer, just as it is for some of them to be more focused on part-time or 'returning' students, or more specialized in providing in-service refresher courses, or more oriented to the needs of their local communities, and so on. By the same token, regimes of funding will have to be diversified, too. The value of these different types of teaching may need to be better reflected and rewarded in the categories by which 'success' is measured. There is an obstructive snobbery behind ignorant sneers at 'mickey-mouse subjects' when the courses in question may be socially valuable forms of applied and vocational training, just as there is an obstructive reverse-snobbery in gibes at 'useless' or 'irrelevant' subjects when the courses in question may involve forms of intellectual enquiry and scholarship that are no less socially valuable. Similarly, what may be appropriate as a way of assessing and funding research in, say, some of the applied sciences that have direct economic impact simply does not work for some of the humanities (indeed, as I argue at several points in this book, it is even doubtful whether the notion of 'research' can be unproblematically used in the latter case). All of these are highly practical matters, and in some cases involve complex financial formulae as well as a labyrinth of monitoring and regulatory requirements. In this book I am not attempting to provide detailed practical alternatives, but I am suggesting that if politicians and administrators do not in the first place have an adequate conception of the activities they are trying to fund and regulate, then their measures will be bound to do damage to the very things they claim to be supporting.

The truth is that the changes that have transformed the landscape of higher education in the past couple of decades have not principally been changes in scholarship and science themselves, but changes in the ways universities are administered, financed, and overseen by their host societies. Public debate overwhelmingly concentrates on these latter aspects, partly just because they are readily intelligible and discussable in ways that the central intellectual activities are not. We need, then, to move on to consider, first, the character of those central intellectual activities, since it is they, after all, that define universities and make them so distinctive; and second, the validity of the various assertions about the functions of these institutions that currently dominate public discussion. We may then be in a position to understand how it is that the ever-rising tide of political and media discussion of this topic gives us so little insight into what universities are *for*.

3

The Useful and the Useless:
Newman Revisited

I

Anyone who attends to the history of debates about the values and purposes of universities needs to cultivate a high tolerance for repetition. The topic's capacity to generate eye-glazing truisms of various kinds seems matched by its tendency to recur to a small set of binary oppositions. In Britain, though also elsewhere, these debates fall into a particularly dispiriting pattern, which might be parodied as the conflict between the 'useful' and the 'useless'. Over and over again since the early nineteenth century, critics, reformers, and governments have claimed that the studies carried on in universities are outdated, irrelevant, or, in a word, useless, and that they need to be made to serve national needs more effectively and more directly – to become, in other words, more useful. For anyone who believes that this conflict expresses a uniquely contemporary set of concerns, I can provide an enlightening, though dauntingly lengthy, reading-list which would reveal that the only really novel element in recent official pronouncements on this matter is the tendency to replace syntax with bullet points.

But why have debates about universities been so repetitive, and repetitive in just this way? Why are the two poles constantly characterized in these simplistic and reductive terms? And while we are asking, we might throw in an obvious follow-up question: namely, why doesn't the 'useful' side of the debate win once and for all? After all, it usually has political or economic power on its side as well as arguments with a ready popular appeal. To hear the familiar cadences about the importance of making the universities 'serve the needs of national life', we have only to go back to the Royal Commissions on Oxford and Cambridge in the mid-Victorian period. These bodies had the political clout to bring about real changes and did so. Nonetheless, the proponents of such arguments have felt it necessary to repeat them pretty much every generation since then. But why, we might wonder, has it been such a Sisyphean task? Irritated politicians and cliché-loving journalists are prone to suggest that it's due to the entrenched conservatism and self-interest of 'the dons'. It's easy to spot this charge coming down the line, since it is invariably preceded by a vacuous reference to 'ivory towers' and often accompanied by a hackneyed gibe about 'swilling port'. But quite apart from its other failings, this is obviously an inadequate explanation, since steps have been taken several times – such as in the 1870s, the 1920s, the 1960s, and the 1980s – to override or break supposed donnish resistance and to use the power of the state to re-orient significant features of higher education. And yet in 2009 the Department of Business, Innovation and Skills still felt the need to issue a document which declared that universities needed to be redirected to make a 'bigger contribution to economic recovery and future growth' and to be 'central to the country's economic performance in the twenty-first century'.

In this chapter I shall explore this question by relating it to another, more minor but in its way no less striking, piece of repetition, namely the constant invocation in the literature on higher education of John Henry Newman's *The Idea of a University*. This book was mainly based on lectures given by Newman in 1852 and addressed to a very specific and now largely forgotten question about establishing a Catholic university in Dublin. And yet, despite these distancing features, the book has remained a constant point of reference in these debates right up to the present. In his recent edition of Newman's book, the American scholar Frank Turner declares: 'No work in the English language has had more influence on the public ideals of higher education.' Indeed, it was described some years ago by Jaroslav Pelikan, himself the author of a notable book about the modern university, as 'the most important treatise on the idea of the university ever written in any language'. The inviolable standing of Newman's book seems beyond doubt, yet its constant re-appearance in modern discussions of universities is – I want, heretically, to suggest – one of the most curious things about these debates.

I say 'heretically' because when a work has become a classic or canonical text, then that status in itself becomes a justification and partial explanation for its subsequent citation – indeed, that is partly what 'classic' and 'canonical' mean in these contexts. Yet it is very far from obvious how or why Newman's mannered and deliberately archaic treatise has achieved and preserved this status, and it is equally unclear quite how it speaks to our present condition. As I have emphasized in earlier chapters, there are now many types of institution to which the label 'university' is applied, and the range of activities carried on within them has expanded dramatically in recent decades, in terms both of courses and of non-academic activity. Robert Maynard Hutchins, the influential President of the University of Chicago in the 1930s and 1940s, once defined a university as a series of schools and departments held together by a central heating system. Clark Kerr, Chancellor of the University of California system a generation later, updated this by suggesting that a university was now best understood as 'a series of individual faculty entrepreneurs held together by a common grievance over parking'. Of course, behind these particular contrasting epigrams, one can see a little climatic or geographical determinism at work. But the diversity of activities carried on in contemporary universities should make us cautious about appearing to follow Newman in finding a single common purpose or identity for these institutions, particularly one that, as I shall explain, derives from a model which essentially pre-dates the establishment of the modern university.

The cumulative changes of recent decades are commonly talked about in terms of the transition from an 'elite' to a 'mass' system of higher education, and there is a tendency, which I think we should resist, to identify 'useless' subjects with the former and 'useful' subjects with the latter. Those who wish, nostalgically or defiantly, to cling to what they believe to be the values of the good old days tend to turn to their Newman for support and comfort. I should make clear, once again, that I do not intend to encourage or endorse that reaction: a properly democratic system of higher education is surely something we should welcome, and anyway it is here to stay. But that makes it all the more difficult to decide in what ways, if any, Newman's ideal can still have any purchase on our current debates.

II

At this point it may be helpful to pause and say a little more about Newman's much-cited but perhaps now little-read book and the circumstances of its origin to bring out just how curious its continuing prominence really is. Newman had been a prominent member of the so-called 'Tractarian' or 'Oxford movement' within the Anglican Church in the 1830s and early 1840s, before finally going over to Rome in 1845. Not only had he attracted considerable suspicion and opprobrium before his conversion for having seemed to stretch the tenets of Anglicanism too far in a Romish direction, but by becoming a Catholic priest, and founding and withdrawing to the Birmingham Oratory, he seemed to be cutting himself off from the main currents of English life and culture at the time. In accepting an invitation from the Irish Catholic hierarchy in 1851 to establish a Catholic university in Dublin, he was undertaking a project which was, under the circumstances, bound to seem a marginal and quixotic endeavour. When, in May 1852, Newman gave the first of the lectures in which he set out his thinking about such an institution, he had to address several kinds of suspicion or scepticism. There was suspicion among the Irish Catholic hierarchy about an institution which might turn out not to be under their direct control. There was scepticism among the Catholic middle class of Dublin that a high-falutin' Oxfordized education would be of any use to their sons. There was scepticism among the noble and wealthy Catholic families of England (whose offspring Newman hoped to attract) about the appeal of an upstart institution that conspicuously lacked social cachet. And there was intense suspicion among the general educated public of Victorian England that a devious and discredited Catholic theologian could be up to any good at all plotting to establish an indoctrination-factory in the capital of England's notoriously troublesome neighbour.

In the event, these and other obstacles did prove too much for Newman and his fledgling institution. It attracted few students; only its medical school really flourished; and before long it was absorbed into the Royal, later the National, University of Ireland, coming in retrospect to be seen as the precursor of what is now University College Dublin. After several attempts in the 1850s to lay down the burden of his office as rector, Newman finally resigned in 1858. The manner of his going was itself expressive of the gap between aspiration and reality: he gave the last of his intellectually and rhetorically ambitious lectures on 4 November 1858, and that very evening he sailed for England, never to return to Ireland in the remaining thirty-two years of his life.

The book we now know as *The Idea of a University* is a composite volume with a complex bibliographic history. The initial lectures which he gave in 1852 he published later that year, together with some further lectures which he wrote but did not deliver, under the title *Discourses on the Scope and Nature of University Education, addressed to the Catholics of Dublin*. In 1858 he published a selection of the addresses he had subsequently given in Dublin in his role as Rector, under the title *Lectures and Essays on University Subjects*. In 1873 he brought the bulk of the contents of these two books together, in revised form, as *The Idea of a University Defined and Illustrated*, which he re-published, with further revisions, in several later editions, culminating in the ninth edition published in 1889, the year before his death. So, the book that has become such a classic began life as a collection of occasional pieces written to justify the creation of a new institution which was somewhat marginal to English social and cultural traditions and which proved to be for the most part a failure. If we ask what it was that enabled Newman's ideas to transcend these unpromising origins, we are invariably referred to two related features of the book itself: first, its defence of the ideal of 'a liberal education'; and second, the seductive charms of Newman's prose.

The three central chapters on a 'liberal education' are frequently excerpted or discussed on their own, but if one reads the *whole* book now with as open a mind as its great reputation permits, one is bound to be struck by its remoteness, its opacity, and, above all, its overriding dogmatic intent. Newman was justifying a Catholic institution to Catholics, and not only is the truth of the Catholic religion an unquestioned datum, but the centrality of theology and correct religious doctrine to the institution he was directing is emphatically insisted upon. Consider just two instances of the difficulties the book may present for many modern readers on this score. First, when he is making the case for the centrality of theology to a university, he insists that 'Religious truth is not only a portion, but a condition of general knowledge,' and that 'Right Reason, that is, Reason rightly exercised, leads the mind to the Catholic faith.' The strict implication of such claims might be that only in a Catholic university constituted along these lines could such general knowledge be properly cultivated. And secondly, when he is exploring the relations between theology and other disciplines, he again makes some very striking assertions. For example, when considering the truth and the status of the theorems of political economy (at the time a topical and much-disputed issue), 'the obvious question which occurs to one to ask', he announces, 'is, what does religion, what does Revelation say on the point? Political Economy must not be allowed to give judgement in its own favour, but must come before a higher tribunal.' Or, more striking still, when discussing the place of subjects such as history in the curriculum, he declares that Revelation furnishes real knowledge which other subjects would be impoverished without: 'Thus, in the science of history, the preservation of our race in Noah's ark is an historical fact, which history never would arrive at without Revelation.'

These, it hardly needs saying, are not the kinds of passage which have most contributed to the book's longevity. Its standing with later secular publics obviously rests on the exposition of the idea of what Newman called 'a liberal education', set out in the three central discourses entitled 'Knowledge its own End', 'Knowledge viewed in relation to Learning', and 'Knowledge viewed in relation to Professional Skill'. And here, as with any interesting and enduring piece of writing, form and content are inseparable. Newman's case in these chapters, that a university provides a liberal not a professional education, is carried, is infiltrated into the reader's mind, less by direct propositional statement and more by the cadences and resonances of a style that combines the oratorical, the liturgical, and the poetic. Through a sequence of beguiling variations, the music of his prose returns to a single refrain: namely, the achievement at which such an education aims is the liberation of the student from all forms of one-sidedness. 'Not to know the relative disposition of things is the state of slaves or children,' he maintains in good Aristotelian fashion. The opposite condition is that produced by a liberal education: 'A habit of mind is formed which lasts through life, of which the attributes are, freedom, equitableness, calmness, moderation, and wisdom; or what in a former Discourse I have ventured to call a philosophical habit.' This curiously heterogeneous list of attributes points to something that falls between an outlook and a character-type, something marked above all by its avoidance of the excited, the passionate, and the partisan. It is akin to what philosophers might call a 'second-order' quality: that is, a disposition towards, or perspective upon, knowledge rather than knowledge of anything in particular, and we shall need to return to this 'contentless' feature of Newman's ideal in a moment.

In starting to subject some of Newman's prose to critical close reading, I would not want to give the impression that I am deaf to its charms or amazed that it has obtained so many admirers in later generations. Who could not thrill to this way of candidly admitting that the qualities inculcated by a liberal education do not necessarily make for moral virtue: 'Quarry the granite rock with razors, or moor the vessel with a thread of silk; then may you hope with such keen and delicate instruments as human knowledge and human reason to contend against those giants, the passions and the pride of man'? Or who could fail to recognize Newman's condemnation of the idea of a university as a mere collocation of disciplines, 'a sort of bazaar, or pantechnicon, in which wares of all kinds are heaped together for sale in stalls independent of each other'? I have to say, however, that there is one sentence in which, however elegant its phrasing, I most emphatically do not recognize my present condition, and that is when he writes: 'There is no situation which combines respectability with lightness of responsibility and labour so happily as the office of a Professor.'

So many of the distinctive features of Newman's case and his own manner of making it are caught by the rhythmical cadences of the paragraph with which he ends his celebrated chapter on 'Knowledge Viewed in Relation to Professional Skill' that it will bear extended quotation. Having insisted that a liberal education does indeed have a practical end in view and that it is nothing less than 'training good members of society', he writes:

> A University training is the great ordinary means to a great but ordinary end; it aims at raising the intellectual tone of society, at cultivating the public mind, at purifying the national taste, at supplying true principles to popular enthusiasm and fixed aims to popular aspiration, at giving enlargement and sobriety to the ideas of the age, at facilitating the exercise of political power, and refining the intercourse of private life. It is the education which gives a man a clear conscious view of his own opinions and judgments, a truth in developing them, an eloquence in expressing them, and a force in urging them. It teaches him to see things as they are, to go right to the point, to disentangle a skein of thought, to detect what is sophistical, and to discard what is irrelevant. It prepares him to fill any post with credit, and to master any subject with facility. It shows him how to accommodate himself to others, how to throw himself into their state of mind, how to bring before them his own, how to influence them, how to come to an understanding with them, how to bear with them. He is at home in any society, he has common ground with every class; he knows when to speak and when to be silent; he is able to converse, he is able to listen; he can ask a question pertinently, and gain a lesson seasonably, when he has nothing to impart himself; he is ever ready, yet never in the way; he is a pleasant companion, and a comrade you can depend upon; he knows when to be serious and when to trifle, and he has a sure tact which enables him to trifle with gracefulness and to be serious with effect . . .

And so it rolls on. Again we cannot help but notice how, in the opening sentence of this extract, the energy and dynamism are assumed to come from outside, from society, and to be potentially dangerous forces, requiring the soothing balm of the university to calm them down. 'Popular enthusiasm' lacks 'true principles', the 'ideas of the age' lack 'sobriety', and so on. Then, as the paragraph proceeds, we move from the qualities which enable a man to fill any position or undertake any task to those qualities which make him agreeable in society.

One ungenerous response such a paragraph might provoke is the thought that something this wonderful liberal education does not teach seems to be a sense of proportion in justifying itself. As Newman's confident incantations sound in our ears, we are bound to find ourselves wondering whether all this does not set the bar a tad high? Can it really be that three years spent in some particular course of study in one's late teens can encompass all this? Newman's language is unnervingly distant from that of a modern 'course aims and objectives' document. Rare must be the contemporary university teacher who in the department handbook declares that the purpose of their course is to produce someone 'who knows when to be serious and when to trifle', and who has 'a sure tact which enables him to trifle with gracefulness and to be serious with effect'. Clearly, what we have here is a statement of *paideia*, an ideal of the shaping of the whole person, the early stages of a life-long course in self-cultivation and character-formation. But more even than this, we are being offered an idealized picture of a type of community, a cross between a Greek *polis*, an aristocratic club, a philosophical seminar, and a cultivated salon. By this point, the university seems to be functioning simply as a metonymy, a location which is somehow exemplary of the ideals of human life as a whole.

Or rather, not life as a whole in Newman's eyes, since, magnificent though his verbal fresco is, this human type is fatally lacking without religion. 'The gentleman', he reminds us, 'is the creation, not of Christianity, but of civilization.' In fact, he insists in a sentence which may surprise some of those who invoke his name, although liberal knowledge 'concurs' with Christianity in some respects, in others it may become what he calls 'an insidious and dangerous foe', and at this point he turns once again to the still higher authority of Revelation, yet another enactment of that recurring tension in his allegiances between the charms of Oxford and the authority of Rome.

But if we confine ourselves for the moment to his case for a liberal education, the lack of proportion or even obvious relation between means and ends may tell us something about the task of justifying universities, and this returns us to the question of the charges or antici-pated reactions against which such a justification is pitched. After all, Newman's virtuoso rhetorical performance in these central chapters was intended to scare off the proponents of utility. Consider, for example, how, having described the cultivation of the mind as the core of a liberal education and thus 'the business of a university', he then goes on in the following passage:

> Now this is what some great men are very slow to allow; they insist that Education should be confined to some particular and narrow end, and should issue in some definite work, which can be weighed and meas-ured. They argue as if every thing, as well as every person, had its price; and that where there has been a great outlay, they have a right to expect a return in kind. This they call making Education and Instruction 'useful,' and 'Utility' becomes their watchword. With a fundamental principle of this nature, they very naturally go on to ask, what there is to show for the expense of a University; what is the real worth in the market of the article called 'a Liberal Education,' on the supposition that it does not teach us definitely how to advance our manufactures, or to improve our lands, or to better our civil economy; or again, if it does not at once make this man a lawyer, that an engineer, and that a sur-geon; or at least if it does not lead to discoveries in chemistry, astronomy, geology, magnetism, and science of every kind.

Here, in easily penetrated disguise, we recognize the forebears of the funding councils and the religion of assessment; here we have antici-pations of that Dickensian (or do I mean Orwellian?) parody of a title, the Department of Business, Innovation and Skills; here we have a ver-sion of the almost comically misconceived quest for 'impact'; here we have early signs of the prioritizing of STEM subjects (science, technol-ogy, engineering, mathematics); and so on. Notice that Newman's prose carefully does not identify his audience or readership with this position: it is ascribed to others, who are kept firmly at bay with the third person plural. A distancing eyebrow is raised at the values evident in such a position: its proponents argue 'as if' their premises were true or on the basis of a 'supposition' about outcomes, and so on. Newman does not yield the high ground, and his ground is very high indeed.

And yet the strategy which he then adopts in response to this critique is extremely curious. Instead of responding directly to these objections, he embarks on a paean of praise to the Oxford college where he had been a fellow, Oriel (which, incidentally, he contrives to present as an essentially Catholic institution), and more particularly to Edward Copleston and John Davison, respectively Provost and Fellow of the college in the early nineteenth century, who took the lead in defending Oxford against the celebrated criticisms advanced in a series of articles in the *Edinburgh Review* between 1808 and 1810. The Edinburgh Reviewers are cast as the voices of utility, and so, extraordinarily, this celebrated chapter, which comes to about sixteen pages in modern editions, devotes seven pages simply to reproducing long passages from the articles by Copleston and Davison. Thus, his case for a liberal education, which is taken to be so resonant still, is not just grounded on, but is expressed in, the terms used to defend what, in the long history of higher education, may seem to be one of the least defensible specimens, namely the unreformed Oxford of the start of the nineteenth century. We may feel that it is already unpromising enough to be trying to justify our activities in the early twenty-first century multiversity by falling back on what a Victorian Catholic theologian had to say when trying to transplant Oxford to Dublin, but it starts to seem almost impossibly recessive when we find him falling back on a still earlier defence of an Oxford that was not far removed from that made notorious by the strictures of Gibbon and Adam Smith. And yet, and yet . . .

Over and over again, Newman's silky prose characterizes the effect of a liberal education not in terms of what students learn or indeed of the acquisition of any particular set of skills, but of the relation in which they come to stand to their knowledge, the manner in which they dispose of it, the perspective they have on the place of their knowledge in a wider map of human understanding. In his most powerful rhetorical flights he goes further still and characterizes the outcome as a way of being, the possession of a certain kind of balance or poise in all of one's conduct. The ideal all this conjures up is beguiling but also, as remarked above, peculiarly contentless. In the structure of Newman's argument, the opposite of being educated is not so much being ignorant as being 'one-sided', in the grip of partial knowledge, over-zealous and lacking in that calm meditativeness which is the mark of philosophic cultivation. The effects Newman ascribes to a liberal education resemble, in this respect, what Matthew Arnold was to say only a few years later about the effect of 'culture' on the individual (and the resemblance is, of course, not accidental, since Arnold drew so heavily on Newman, not least in the elusive matter of tone).

One reason for the longevity of Newman's book may be precisely that he does not tie the justification of a university to any particular subject-matter or canon, which might, of course, quickly become outdated. He clearly assumes that a central place will be occupied by traditional genteel studies such as philosophy, classics, and history, all under the overarching jurisdiction of theology. But by couching his justification in terms of manner or tone, of a relation rather than a content, he provides a rhetoric which is portable, adaptable to a variety of cultural and educational traditions. And it allows the benefits of a liberal education to coexist with a great variety of subsequent occupations in a way in which a skill- or content-based justification could not do. 'A cultivated intellect,' he declares, 'because it is a good in itself, brings with it a power and a grace to every work and occupation which it undertakes, and enables us to be more useful, and to a greater number.' Clearly, those last two phrases are intended to turn the flank of the demand for usefulness, offering a higher or more encompassing form of utility. But again, this falls back on something elusively general: an education in no matter what equips a man to do no matter what.

The question of what I am calling the excessiveness of Newman's case may be addressed from another angle. As I have already suggested, the more stirring and encompassing the terms in which his ideal of a liberal education is described, the less plausible becomes the suggestion that these virtues will be acquired by spending three years in one's late teens studying a particular subject. But we should also remark that the realities of the English universities in the first half of the nineteenth century would have made such an outcome yet more implausible for two further reasons.

First, these great ends were to be encompassed by being subjected to a narrow range of traditional exercises involving the Greek and Latin languages and certain aspects of mathematics, principally Euclidean geometry. In practice, this narrow curriculum resembled a form of mental gymnastics rather than an introduction to a cultural inheritance. Copleston made this the nub of his defence against the strictures of the Edinburgh Reviewers; precisely because these studies had no content which could be applied to the contemporary world, they trained the mind for its own sake. Here we have again what I earlier referred to as the peculiarly 'contentless' character of this educational ideal. Moreover, as Newman's sonorous periods echo in our ears – what is acquired by the student, we are told, is 'a faculty of judgment, of clear-sightedness, of sagacity, of wisdom, of philosophical reach of mind, and of intellectual self-possession and repose' – we cannot help but think that a lot is being expected of a facility for turning English verse into Latin epigrams. A similar mismatch between means and ends seems always to dog the statement of this case.

Second, not only did many of the riotous young gentlemen and dim clergymen who emerged from this process in the early mid-nineteenth century seem rather strikingly to lack the qualities it was alleged to cultivate, but (the other side of this coin) Newman appeared to be suggesting that human and intellectual qualities which were so fundamental as to be almost universal could *only* be acquired by those who happened to, and could afford to, submit themselves to a regime that was exclusively available in two small English market towns. So necessary to the acquisition of this philosophic capacity does he appear to make a period of residence in one of these peculiar institutions that one can only wonder at how most of those figures from the past whose intellectual or cultural achievements Newman himself celebrates elsewhere in his writings ever struggled out of the mire of one-sidedness and a general lack of mental flexibility. And once again, the same excess lurks in even the best-intentioned defences of universities today, to the point where the sceptic begins to wonder at the implication that reflective or analytical capacities can *only* arise and survive as the result of a successful UCAS application.

In all these ways, the task of justifying universities seems inexorably to lead to rhetorical overkill. So what are we to make of the excess in Newman's argument, the glaring disproportion between the means and the end? In the shoot-out with the proponents of 'utility', his fire-power seems not just superior but of a different order of magnitude. Like a good debater, he ends the paragraph I have been quoting from by reminding the reader that the conclusive victory he has just won has been fought on the enemy's turf: 'The art which tends to make a man all this, is in the object which it pursues as useful as the art of wealth or the art of health.' I began by asking how it is that the proponents of utility didn't long ago win the conflict once and for all, but by the end of Newman's most celebrated chapter one wonders that they have ever had the temerity, faced with the massed artillery of the Hellenized Western tradition, even to raise their risible squeak.

But isn't this, too, a recognizable feature of the recurring clash between the useful and the useless? Aren't the defenders of the latter *always* being driven into a kind of overstatement? The terms in which the non-instrumental case is couched – the case, as it is often now put, for education rather than mere training – seem inexorably driven to ambitious phrases about the most general and most desirable human qualities, about a vision of a civilized community, about the ends of life. In the abstract, these may be thought to trump claims about equipping the workforce or increasing the GDP, though it is bound to be something of a hollow victory, since the two types of justification belong to such different orders of discourse. But, more than that, the difficulty with this argument today is similar to the problem I identified a moment ago in Newman's case: it is hard to see how the soaring ambitiousness of the outcome is produced given the necessarily limited character of the means. And for that reason, the goals may not seem to entail the teaching of any particular subject-matter. After all, the study of very diverse kinds of material may encourage students to become more analytical or more discerning or more articulate, so such outcomes cannot in themselves provide a sufficient justification for learning about, say, Carolingian monarchs or Milton's verse-forms rather than something else.

III

I want now briefly to pursue a parallel line of thought. One of the lessons to be drawn from the history of universities which I sketched in Chapter 2 is that subjects which were initially introduced for broadly practical purposes have outlived those purposes and gone on to establish themselves as scholarly disciplines in their own right. This, it could be said, is in some respects the story of the classics, in their long journey from being a preparation for clerical or political office, through the centuries in which they served to hallmark a gentleman, and on to their current standing as favoured example of a 'useless' subject. But something similar might be said about history, seen by its Victorian champions as a practical training for statesmen and administrators, but now a far-flung academic empire with numberless provinces undreamed of a century or more ago; or indeed of subjects such as Oriental languages or anthropology, devised to train the colonial administrator but now elaborated into a number of enterprises defined in purely academic terms. And perhaps we see something broadly similar at work in our own day with subjects such as social policy or education, which initially became subjects for teaching and research with severely practical ends in view, but which have now spawned all the disciplinary paraphernalia of theoretical debate, dedicated journals, and so on. This pattern highlights one of the key differences between universities and superficially similar organisms such as the research and development arms of commercial companies or various political and pressure-group think-tanks. Institutions of these latter kinds pursue enquiry into a topic for a strictly practical purpose, defined by external criteria, and if enquiry no longer serves that purpose then it is abandoned. Moreover, they are not interested in what we might call second-order enquiries into the boundaries of the topic, or the character of the vocabulary being employed, or the status of the knowledge produced. One mark of an academic discipline is that such second-order enquiries can never be deemed illegitimate or irrelevant in advance, and when reflection is free to proceed without the imperative to contribute to a specific external purpose, such second-order questions inevitably start to exert their seductive attraction.

And this point may here be brought into connection with another feature of the history of higher education in this country (which I also touched upon in Chapter 2): namely, the tendency for institutions which were set up to provide some kind of alternative to the model of the existing universities, such as the early 'civic' universities or the Colleges of Advanced Technology or the polytechnics, to come over time to adopt many features of that dominant model. In addition, universities which attempted to break the mould in other ways, such as Keele in the 1950s or some of the so-called 'plate-glass' universities such as Sussex in the 1960s, have in time abandoned most of what made them revolutionary or distinctive in favour of the prevailing model of single-subject department-based degrees. So the pattern of both disciplinary and institutional development exhibits features of what has been called 'academic drift'. Clearly, it is not just the self-interest or professional ambition of individual scholars which brings this about, and here we approach the question of the repeated clash between the useful and the useless from another angle.

For, in emphasizing the repetitiveness of these debates I am not suggesting that there have been no significant historical changes. Overall, we can see how the persistence of what we might call broadly pre-capitalist cultural attitudes through the nineteenth and into the early twentieth century helped sustain a public discourse in which the values associated with the traditional elites could be appealed to in justifying the idea of a liberal education. Snobbery and social exclusiveness played their part here. Across the second half of the twentieth century, the dominant discourse became, successively, more democratic, more utilitarian, more economistic, and now more populist. It is hardly surprising if universities, which, as I have just indicated, have at least in part been displaying the recurring urge to move in more purely academic directions, should have come to be regarded as recalcitrant or backward-looking. This helps account for some of the irritation detectable in successive spokesmen for government and industry: 'Surely', they say, 'these changes have been made before, yet here, in our hour of economic need, the universities have again been backsliding into uselessness.'

Here we begin to touch on a deeper level of explanation for the recurring contest between the useful and useless. Intellectual enquiry is in itself ungovernable: there is no predicting where thought and analysis may lead when allowed to play freely over almost any topic, as the history of science abundantly illustrates. It is sometimes said that in universities knowledge is pursued 'for its own sake', but that may mis-describe the variety of purposes for which different kinds of understanding may be sought. A better way to characterize the intellectual life of universities may be to say that the drive towards understanding can never accept an arbitrary stopping-point, and critique may always in principle reveal that any currently accepted stopping-point *is* ultimately arbitrary. Human understanding, when not chained to a particular instrumental task, is restless, always pushing onwards, though not in a single or fixed or entirely knowable direction, and there is no one moment along that journey where we can say in general or in the abstract that the degree of understanding being sought has passed from the useful to the useless.

In other words, it is not the subject-matter itself that determines whether something is, at a particular moment, classed as 'useful' or 'useless'. Almost any subject can fall under either description. Rather, it is a question of whether enquiry into that subject is being undertaken under the sign of limitlessness – that is to say, not just, as with the development of all knowledge, subject to the testing of hypotheses or the revision of errors, but where the open-ended quest for understanding has primacy over any application or intermediate outcome. This, we might say, is one mark of an academic discipline, and for this reason attempts to make universities into a type of institution where scholars and students study only what is 'useful' are bound, eventually, to end in a kind of failure. The attempt itself can do untold damage, of course, and I am not proposing we should take much comfort from this thought. But all endeavours after systematic understanding of some particular subject-matter are prone to generate further reflections on the limitations or premises of that understanding which cannot themselves be entirely corralled or subordinated to present uses. Moreover, present uses soon become outdated, but the forms of enquiry they provoked do not, or at least they get absorbed into continuing larger enquiries. From time to time, efforts will be made by governments or other representatives of the presumed 'needs of society' to redirect these energies in some currently favoured practical direction, which partly accounts for the continuing gavotte danced by proponents of the 'useful' against the 'useless'.

A university, it may be said, is a protected space in which various forms of useful preparation for life are undertaken in a setting and manner which encourages the students to understand the contingency of any particular packet of knowledge and its interrelations with other, different forms of knowledge. To do this, the teachers themselves need to be engaged in constantly going beyond the confines of the packets of knowledge that they teach, and there is no way to prescribe in advance what will and will not be fruitful ways to do that. Undergraduate education involves exposing students for a while to the experience of enquiry into something in particular, but enquiry which has no external goal other than improving the understanding of that subject-matter. One rough and ready distinction between university education and professional training is that education relativizes and constantly calls into question the information which training simply transmits. In this sense, education encourages the student to recognize the ways in which particular bits of knowledge are not fixed or eternal or universal or self-sufficient. That may be done about almost any subject-matter, though it can only be done through engagement with some *particular* subject-matter, not simply by ingesting a set of abstract propositions about the contingency of knowledge, and the more there already exists an elaborated and sophisticated tradition of enquiry in a particular area, the more demanding and rigorous will be the process of acquiring and revising understanding. What Newman called 'a liberal education' has become a figure or metonym for this surplus over and above training for an occupation.

One way to think about the rhetorical excess of Newman's defence of a liberal education, then, is to see it as a by-product of the attempt to capture, or at least to symbolize, that quality of understanding that is the opposite of all forms of what he, in a familiar spatial metaphor, termed 'one-sidedness'. We cannot adequately or easily describe what happens to the mind when it is 'enlarged' (one of our most common metaphors for the process) by engagement with a series of 'wider perspectives' (another spatial metaphor). By the same token we cannot easily say what is involved in that collective enlargement of understanding that happens when a topic is treated as part of an academic discipline, though once again we tend to use spatial terms about 'fields' or 'branches' of knowledge. Being able to see something 'from all sides' or 'in the round' cannot, by definition, be a specialism in its own right, though it may be thought of as a potential which lurks in all reflective understanding. It is a potential that can only ever be partially realized, since any intellectual framework (yet another spatial or structural metaphor, incidentally) can always be dismantled or absorbed into a yet wider frame.

Newman, of course, concentrates on the education of the undergraduate and the characteristics of the liberally educated man, but the language which he uses to describe this outcome returns again and again to this movement from the narrow to the broad, from the closed to the open, from the fixed to the fluid. One rough abridgement of his case would be to say that a university is a place where this movement is not just tolerated but is the animating principle of the institution. And perhaps the conveying of some sense of this illimitability of enquiry is part of what we might now mean by our equivalent of Newman's 'liberal education', stripped of its class associations and freed from the anyway incompatible constraints of dogmatic theology. We might re-cast some of his majestic cadences into propositions, more modest in tone but no less ambitious in their reach, about trying to give students some sense of the contingency or vulnerability of the knowledge that is, in other settings, treated as so fixed and stable.

Obviously, from this distance Newman's ideal cannot help but seem highly class- and gender-bound, geared to socializing young gentlemen into the obligations of their station. Consistent with this is the emphasis he places on residence and social intercourse among the students, and his dismissal of an urban university such as London as a glorified degree factory, in which students may attend some lectures but essentially just prepare for examinations. His ideal clearly presumes features of an idealized Oxford college of the early nineteenth century, an institution which could persuade itself that a little character-formation among the future governing elite was intrinsically and not just contingently bound up with the cultivation of intellectual enquiry by a small society of leisured savants. Snobbish emulation of this ideal has surely fuelled some of that aggressive-defensive disdain for mere usefulness which has been a tiresome and discreditable feature of the traditionalists' case, as in the Victorian jingle composed in response to the foundation of the new civic universities in major provincial cities:

> He gets degrees in making jam
> At Liverpool and Birmingham.

However, none of this, as I mentioned earlier, seems to have prevented Newman's book being cited by those wishing to defend the kind of research and examining institution which each generation of new institutions has, over time, striven to become – and which he would have scorned.

For a piece of what we awkwardly call 'non-fiction prose' to last, and speak to later generations, it needs to have the power of an individual voice and the passion which comes from arguing a particular case. It must have that intensity of compositional energy, those sparks of wit or anger that are the trace-marks of an individual sensibility feeling its way to the heart of an issue. The circumstances of the particular case are bound to change, the immediate passions to fade, but some such engagement may be necessary to provoke the author to the general statement. No one in the future is going to re-read and be inspired by an administrator's sequence of bullet points or by a 'mission statement' composed by committee. If we think of some of the other classics of Victorian prose in whose company Newman's *Idea of a University* belongs, such as Arnold's *Culture and Anarchy* or Mill's *On Liberty* or Ruskin's *Unto This Last*, they all illustrate the dynamic whereby passionate engagement with a set of contemporary arguments stirs the author's eloquence into something that transcends those polemics, even though his response may be initially cast in the form of occasional lectures or articles. This pattern may tell us something about one way of producing some worthwhile statement of the case for universities in our own time.

IV

After Newman returned from Ireland for the last time in 1858, he spent the remaining thirty-two years of his life in the Birmingham Oratory, which by then had moved to Edgbaston. Only two years after Newman issued his *Idea of a University* as a book in 1873, the industrialist Josiah Mason established Mason College of Science in that city, the forerunner of what became the University of Birmingham (itself now sited in Edgbaston), the first university in Britain to have a Faculty of Commerce. This combination of geographical propinquity and cultural distance may be allowed to stand for Newman's relation to the vast subsequent expansion of higher education in Britain, where he has remained the slightly shadowy, reclusive figure down the road, a haunting, reproachful presence in a system of higher education largely given over to purposes he thought inimical to the true idea of a university.

But a presence nonetheless. I was interested to learn from a recent study of Mark Pattison, the Oxford figure who is often taken to represent an alternative conception of a university as a home for the research ideal, that 'on the mantelpiece of his study Pattison kept, to the end of his life, a framed photograph of Newman.' British universities have kept a framed photograph of Newman on their mantelpieces for 150 years now, partly, as with most mantelpieces, to show off the classiness of their social connections; partly as a memento of more idealistic days, rather like an invitation to a college reunion; partly to avoid the protests that would follow from removing it; partly just to hide the cracks in the wall they cannot afford to have repaired.

I have suggested that we should not delude ourselves into thinking that *The Idea of a University* describes an institution that at all closely resembles the universities we have today or that it provides us with arguments which are likely to be readily effective in their defence. But poetry, oratory, and liturgy can all have in common the power to stir us into recognition of something that we cannot quite name, and the remarkable longevity of Newman's book, which exhibits features of all three genres, suggests it still retains some of this power. The twenty-first century university needs a literary voice of comparable power to articulate in the idiom of our own time the ideal of the untrammelled quest for understanding, but until such a work is written, we have good reason to keep the photograph on the mantelpiece.

4
The Character of the Humanities

In contemporary public discussion of universities, it invariably proves more difficult to characterize the nature of teaching and research in the humanities, and thus to explain their value, than it does to give such an account of the scientific, medical, and technological disciplines. In reality, public understanding of these latter disciplines may be no more informed or accurate than it is of the humanities, but a familiar and easily graspable case can be made in terms of 'discovering' truths about the natural world and then applying those discoveries to better the human condition. A no less cogent case can, of course, be made about the importance of understanding the human world, though it is misleading if this is couched exclusively in terms of discovering new truths, and anyway the immediate benefits of such improved understanding are harder to specify briefly. As a result, public statements about the humanities, in particular, tend to fall back on a sequence of abstract nouns which, though they are in some sense both appropriate and accurate, always risk the danger of sounding pious and lifeless.

A further difficulty is that in present circumstances any invitation to *characterize* the work of scholars in the humanities is almost immediately construed as a demand to *justify* it. It is true that all descriptions will have elements of valuation built into them, and so any characterization can be made to serve the purposes of justification. But there is, as I have suggested, an inescapable element of defensiveness in all attempts to vindicate one's activity – an assumption that the demand issues from unsympathetic premises and an anticipation of resistance or dismissiveness on the part of those who do not share our starting-points. This chapter is not written in that spirit. Instead, it attempts to explore, in relatively informal terms, what actually goes on in the humanities, and what the practice of at least some of these disciplines is like (the practice I shall concentrate on is the activity of scholarship rather than of teaching, though that boundary is not as clear-cut as is often assumed). A few common misconceptions will be challenged along the way, but only in its final section, once such a characterization has been put in place, does the chapter directly address the vexed issue of how best to go about 'defending' the humanities.

Perhaps the most important single thing to say in this context about work in the humanities is that it is in many ways not so different from work in the natural and social sciences. The effort to understand and explain that is at the heart of all scholarly and scientific enquiry is governed by broadly similar canons of accuracy and precision, of rigour in argument and clarity in presentation, of respect for the evidence and openness to criticism, and so on. Biologists may, in their own way, examine the relevant evidence no less systematically and dispassionately than, in their own way, do historians; physicists may use concepts and forms of notation which are, in their own way, every bit as abstract and precise as those deployed by philosophers. All kinds of distinctions can be drawn among various disciplines and groups of disciplines in terms of method, subject-matter, outcomes, and so on, but these distinctions do not all map neatly on to one another so as to fall into two mutually exclusive groups. And all disciplines involve, ultimately, a similar drive towards open-ended understanding, so, for that reason, all disciplines have a stake in the well-being of the university. One reason to be cautious about isolating the humanities for separate discussion is that it can seem to encourage lazy notions of there being 'two cultures', and most versions of that hackneyed claim are misleading and obstructive.

Of course, for various institutional and practical purposes certain disciplines have to be grouped together, though we should be aware, first, that the lines of division are drawn differently not just in different countries but even in different universities within the same country, and, second, that these groupings have changed over time. At present, 'the humanities' represents one such pragmatic grouping, but it is worth noting that this arrangement, and this use of the label, are both comparatively recent. The nineteenth century mostly operated with several more traditional terms, such as 'letters' or (in more theorized or self-conscious settings) 'the moral sciences'; in time, British universities came to use 'arts' as the convenient organizational antonym for 'sciences'. 'The humanities', a term not very widely used in that century, generally connoted the study of the Classics, and 'Humanity' in the singular could be used as a synonym for Latin literature (in some Scottish universities the Professor of Latin was known as the 'Professor of Humanity' into the second half of the twentieth century). The use of the plural term in its contemporary sense gained currency in the USA in the middle decades of the twentieth century, especially as part of a response to an aggressive form of positivism that promoted the supposed methods of the natural sciences as the basis for all true knowledge. This usage became increasingly widespread in Britain in the course of the 1940s and 1950s: the appearance in 1964 of a 'Pelican Original' entitled *Crisis in the Humanities* provoked discussion of various kinds, but the use of that collective label was by then uncontroversial. However, this brief history signals two related themes which have remained characteristic of so much discourse about the humanities: first, it has been largely reactive and has thus tended to have a defensive or vindicatory edge to it in a way not true of most discourse about 'the sciences'; and secondly, the humanities turn out to be almost always in 'crisis'. There has been a good deal of writing under that heading in the USA in the past decade, and a similar urge to draw the wagons into a circle is evident in the humanities departments of British universities at present in response to recent government policies.

The current edition of the *OED* defines this usage of 'the humanities' as follows: 'The branch of learning concerned with human culture; the academic subjects collectively comprising this branch of learning, as history, literature, ancient and modern languages, law, philosophy, art, and music.' This rightly makes the academic location of the term primary, and its illustrative list of disciplines would not cause too many eyebrows to be raised, though it might need saying that art and music are normally only included when understood as objects of scholarly study – as, for example, in art history or musicology – rather than as forms of creative practice. Going beyond lexicography, it may be helpful to say that the label 'the humanities' is now taken to embrace that collection of disciplines which attempt to understand, across barriers of time and culture, the actions and creations of other human beings considered as bearers of meaning, where the emphasis tends to fall on matters to do with individual or cultural distinctiveness and not on matters which are primarily susceptible to characterization in purely statistical or biological terms. This may be a better way of putting it than the rather hackneyed distinction between studying the human as opposed to the physical world: disciplines such as demography or neuropsychology deal with human beings, but only incidentally with individuals or groups as bearers of meanings, and it is for that reason that we would not normally include them under the heading of the humanities. This formula does not allow a hard-and-fast distinction to be drawn between the humanities and the social sciences: several of the disciplines usually classed among the latter exhibit an interpretive or cultural dimension as well as more theoretical or quantitative characteristics – this is true, in different ways, of such disciplines as politics, anthropology, and archaeology. Sometimes the same subject-matter may be part of the inheritance of fields on either side of the notional fence: political thought is studied by intellectual historians as well as by political scientists; past social behaviour is grist to the sociologist as well as to the social historian. Linguistics, a particular problem for tidy-minded classifiers, has some common ground with historians of language and even with literary critics, yet it also shares some approaches with experimental psychology and acoustics.

One response to the porousness and instability of the boundaries of 'the humanities' is to seek to restrict the term to some kind of indisputable heartland, confining the label to the study of the masterpieces of Western thought and literature. This response is particularly evident in some recent discussions of the role of the humanities in the United States, where the focus has been on pedagogy, with a tendency to issue in justifications of 'great books' courses. But to restrict the term in this way flies in the face of what is now established usage, as well as being undesirable on other, practical grounds. The label needs to encompass the whole body of learning and exact scholarship that has been built up in the study of ancient and modern languages, of various forms of history, of art, music, religion and culture generally, in the past and the present, not just the works of the great writers and philosophers.

All this may seem to be a matter of taxonomy – important for those with something at stake in being part of one category rather than another, but inevitably rather arid and lifeless when viewed from further away. Nonetheless, it may be helpful to be reminded at the outset of the diversity of types of work grouped together as the humanities, since most general statements about that category tend to have a flattening effect, representing the forms of enquiry as more uniform than they actually are. A quick visit to the relevant sections of a good academic library reveals how dissimilar, even in its appearance on the page, scholarship in these different areas can be. From the numbered propositions or symbol-strewn sentences of short journal articles in philosophy, through the cumulative and extensively footnoted arrangement of empirical evidence in a 500-page work of history, and on to a collection of stylish essays in literary criticism – the forms of work in the humanities are almost as diverse as the cultural and temporal variety of their subject-matter.

Faced with shelf after shelf of books and articles on what may seem to be a limited and repetitive range of topics, the lay reader is prone to wonder what there can possibly be left to say. Surely by now scholars know all there is to know about Shakespeare or the causes of the French Revolution or the arguments for freedom of the will. Granted that in a few cases genuinely new evidence may come to light, as the lucky scholar stumbles on a hitherto-unknown work that had been mis-catalogued or tracks down a suitcase of revealing letters in the dusty attic of some famous person's descendant. But mostly, muses the lay reader, scholars seem to be writing about the same texts, the same material, the same problems as their predecessors have been doing for, in some areas, many generations. So what exactly are they *doing*?

What they, we, are doing much of the time is worrying. The default condition of the scholar is one of intellectual dissatisfaction. No matter how exhilarating it may be to discover new evidence or come up with an illuminatingly apt characterization, one can never (and perhaps should never) entirely banish the sense that the current state of one's work can only ever have the status of an interim report, always vulnerable to being challenged, corrected, or simply bypassed. The mind searches for pattern, for a kind of order, but this is a restless, endless process. One of the things that can make a book influential in the humanities – and it is usually a book, since a fairly wide canvas is needed to display the pattern in all its persuasive detail – is that the pattern which it proposes becomes the framework for much subsequent scholarship in the particular area. Obvious examples of books which shaped a whole sub-field a generation or more ago might include E. P. Thompson's *The Making of the English Working Class* (1963), or Frank Kermode's *The Sense of an Ending* (1967), or John Rawls's *A Theory of Justice* (1971), and in some respects those works never lose their pertinence. However, not only are such books subjected to more or less constant criticism and revision (including by their own authors), but there is a sense in which a particular scholarly community simply moves on – moves on to other topics, or to using different methods, or to asking new questions. That it does so is not entirely a matter of the discovery of new empirical evidence or the operation of intellectual fashion or shifting pressures from the outside world, though these can all have a part to play. It is, more fundamentally, because no starting-point is beyond re-consideration, because no assumptions (about how societies change or how people act or how meanings mean) are beyond challenge, because no vocabulary has an exclusive monopoly. And this is where that existential state of intellectual dissatisfaction turns into something like a methodological precept. It will, in practice, require experienced judgement to decide at what point asking a different kind of question is a fruitful way to proceed and when it is simply going to be obstructive or irrelevant. But in principle no question can be ruled out in advance. Someone else can always start from somewhere else – and so, therefore, can we. There can only ever be interim reports.

This is one of the places where insisting on the difference between knowledge and understanding becomes vital. How we understand a particular topic depends, among other things, on what else we already understand. The point here is akin to that made long ago about the search for authenticity in the so-called 'early music' movement: we may play the pieces on period instruments but we cannot listen to them with period ears. Part of the reason why we, now, cannot understand Shakespeare in exactly the same way as, say, A. C. Bradley did in his classic work on *Shakespearean Tragedy* (1904) is not just because our knowledge of that particular writer has advanced, but because our understanding of so much else has changed. It is true that we know more now than we did a century ago about, for example, the transmission of Shakespeare's texts or about the conditions of Elizabethan stagecraft. But, more fundamentally, we have encountered different ideas about matters as various as the operation of ethnic stereotyping or the social subordination of women as well as about the interpretation of character in drama in general or even about the relation between writing and meaning. In some respects, scholarship attempts to come as close as we can to acquiring period ears, to become more and more familiar with the language and assumptions of the period in which a work was written. But, still, it is *we* who are doing the understanding, and we are trying to communicate that understanding to a contemporary audience in a contemporary idiom. We couldn't simply repeat the perceptions and judgements of a hundred years ago even if we tried.

One of the most striking illustrations of the way in which starting from somewhere else can result in a rich harvest of new insights and interpretations is the transforming effect that attending to questions of gender and sexuality has had on so many areas of scholarship in the past three decades. In its most obvious form this has brought whole bodies of previously neglected or unknown material into focus. For example, every literary scholar's awareness of the range of significant writing by women in earlier centuries has been extended in ways never imagined a couple of generations ago, just as there are now whole areas of social and cultural history which barely existed before historians began systematically to quiz the evidence from earlier centuries about the activities of that half of the population which scarcely figured in many public records. But such a change of perspective can inspire new work in less obvious ways, too. For instance, some moral and political philosophers began to ask themselves questions about the implicitly male characteristics of the standpoint from which agency is assessed or about the gendered nature of certain measures of well-being. Not all the claims and re-interpretations that have resulted from asking this particular set of questions have stood up to subsequent examination, any more than have those issuing from other kinds of broadly revisionist surges, but the landscape of scholarship across the humanities has been decisively modified in ways that seem unlikely simply to disappear in the future.

Even if all this is granted, and all the new topics and perspectives are acknowledged as legitimate extensions of the range and interpretive power of scholarship, still the outside observer is prone to feel that an awful lot of the energy of scholars in the humanities does not seem to be directed to discovering new material but instead to controverting other scholars. And this is not just a matter of correcting particular mistakes of fact or errors of interpretation, but rejection of the other scholars' whole approach. How can it be, it is asked, that disciplines that have existed in some form for decades or even for centuries have not yet managed to resolve the most basic issues of approach and method? Actually, the conclusion drawn from this observation of continuing dispute is exaggerated. Even members of rival 'schools' within a particular discipline share a hugely greater area of agreement, often unspoken, about legitimate procedures and established truths than the headline-grabbing confrontation over points of difference might suggest. But still, there simply is a lot of fundamental dispute within the humanities, and perhaps the proper response to this fact is not to see these disciplines as failed sciences (not that such disagreement is absent from the sciences either), but to recognize how closely work in these fields is bound up with the most fundamental aspects of being human. It scarcely surprises us that there is no one agreed account of what it is to live a life or indeed that there is no agreed way adequately to frame that issue as a topic for enquiry in the first place, and it should, therefore, not surprise us that all attempts to understand aspects of human life, past or present, no matter how disciplined they may be in their analysis of concepts and their handling of evidence, will reproduce some of this fundamental lack of agreement.

One way to understand the role of what is now often referred to simply as 'theory' in the literary and historical disciplines is to say that 'theory' is what happens when common starting-points can no longer be taken for granted. For example, literary critics in the English-speaking world in the 1950s and 1960s disagreed about many things – about the authorship of certain Jacobean plays or about the influence of Keats on Tennyson or about whether D. H. Lawrence was a great writer – but for the most part they did not disagree about whether the evaluation of literary worth was legitimate or even possible, or indeed about whether there was such a category as 'literature'. When all these concepts and procedures are defamiliarized, made to seem culturally contingent rather than logically necessary, debate has to move to a more theoretical or abstract level. But once again, this is not a form of pathology, not something that happens because there is nothing more to say about the established canon or because literary scholars have lost interest in literature (though some may have). It may, rather, be an index of health, or at least a sign that scholars cannot and should not be immune to the intellectual changes consequent upon living in a more diverse society in which the assumptions shared by certain traditional elites no longer command general assent.

And something like this is also the proper response to the charge repeatedly levelled against the humanities in recent decades, particularly but not exclusively by right-wing commentators, that scholarship has been 'corrupted' by being 'politicized'. For there can be no understanding of human history and human self-expression that does not work with categories and concepts that have a political dimension. Where a dominant discourse is unchallenged, these political dimensions can be allowed to remain implicit, effectively invisible, but they are still there. Within particular areas of scholarship, these issues may be bracketed off, set aside, or merely taken for granted. The drive of theoretical critique is to bring such matters to the surface and to make *them* the focus of attention. Once again, explicit attention to long-unchallenged premises can be made to appear as the illegitimate introduction into scholarly exchange of matters that do not belong there, but most often such critique is a way of registering the pressure of wider social and cultural changes on the always restless, never settled, attempt to expand understanding.

The fact that scholarship in the humanities must, at least in part, deploy the language of everyday description is, paradoxically, one source of another recurring complaint by journalists, reviewers, and others. This complaint assumes, partly because of the presence of such everyday language, that all work in the humanities should be readily intelligible to non-specialist readers, and so when it encounters various forms of specialized professional discourse it cries foul. Because most of the individual words look familiar, it is assumed that the meanings of the sentences and paragraphs which they help to make up should be readily intelligible as well. And of course in many cases, particularly in historical and literary subjects, they are. But it is part of the search for precision in any field to attempt to use terms in carefully specified senses, and after a while there will be no need to remind fellow-specialists that a term is being used in that sense because it has become second nature to all those who spend their working lives reading such material. Readers coming from outside – from outside that discipline, which may not mean from outside the university; we are all non-specialists in relation to all other fields – may be at first misled into assuming that a particular term (and others like it) is being used in its familiar sense and may then quickly become resentful on finding that what they thought was an inviting path is in practice an impenetrable thicket. This then feeds into the larger charge, which in turn has a long history, that specialization has gone 'too far' and academic scholarship in the humanities has cut itself off from the 'general reader'. For the most part, this reproach is not now levelled at those working in the natural sciences, or even many of the social sciences: it is accepted that the non-specialist cannot expect to be able to read an article published in a professional journal in, say, molecular biology or atomic physics, and that the highly technical nature of the writing is a commendable sign that scientists in those fields have pushed far beyond what common sense or casual observation could achieve – indeed, that that is part of what we understand 'science' to mean. But the premise implicit in the recurrent reproach to scholarship in the humanities, by contrast, seems to be that any description of human activity should be readily intelligible to any reasonably well-educated reader, or in other words that the humanities' subject-matter should entail this requirement of general intelligibility. Actually, there is no good reason to accept this premise: human activity may be made the object of enquiries that are just as technical or statistical or abstract as any other subject-matter, and in these areas as in others the form of expression taken by the results of those enquiries will be determined by professional norms, intended readership, and so on.

These issues are further complicated by the patterns of publishing associated with various disciplines. All working scientists expect to publish the results of their latest research in a number of highly specialized journals (whether print or electronic), journals which no outsider would ever be likely to encounter let alone assume would make agreeable reading. A few of those scientists may also have a gift or inclination for popularization, and they may then write in an utterly different idiom in trying to summarize and communicate the interest of a wide body of research in their field to a 'general reader'. But the two genres are entirely divorced from each other, and no biologist or physicist or chemist, qua biologist or physicist or chemist, ever builds a successful career except through specialized publishing of the first kind. (There are now a small number of posts devoted to the 'public understanding' of science, where work of the second kind may be the appropriate form of professional publishing, but that is separate from the practice of any scientific discipline in itself.) Much the same is now true in several of the social sciences: for example, many economists or social psychologists may only ever publish articles in professional journals. This can be true in certain areas of the humanities: many philosophers publish exclusively in this form, as do some historical demographers and musicologists. But in other fields – especially, say, political and military history, but also literary biography and art history – books are published which aim simultaneously to meet the needs of both specialist and non-specialist readers. A historian of the Second World War, for example, might build a highly respected academic career chiefly on the basis of publishing books which, though they draw on original research and meet the stiffest requirements of scholarly rigour, can also be given as Christmas presents.

In practice, this avenue is open to very few scholars even among historians, and it is not an option for most academics in other fields, including literary criticism (literary biography is another matter). But the structure of publishing, particularly in the UK, still encourages the idea that a book on a historical or literary topic is somehow defective if it cannot be read with pleasure by an uninstructed reader. Of course, it is not the case that 'specialist' and 'general' readers are two mutually exclusive and exhaustive categories: some works of scholarship may be read by those in adjoining fields, by those in other fields, and occasionally by those who cultivate no scholarly field. And, of course, these categories and boundaries change over time: for a while in the 1950s and 1960s even quite rarefied works of literary criticism enjoyed a considerable *réclame*. And such boundaries are drawn in different ways in different cultures: some works of philosophy or anthroplogy, for example, can still expect successfully to address *le grand public* in France and several other Latin countries. But for the most part scholarship in the humanities, like work in all other academic disciplines, is principally addressed to fellow-specialists, and quite properly so.

II

Having begun with these general and somewhat abstract considerations about the humanities disciplines, I now want to look at aspects of professional activity in these fields in a more concrete manner. We may begin with an extremely obvious point about everyday practice in the life of a scholar in the humanities: at every level we are called upon to make judgements of quality, judgements whose grounds remain for the most part beyond conclusive demonstration. That is to say, we are constantly in the business of trying to distinguish outstanding from merely good work and good work from the mediocre or unacceptable. This is as true of us in our roles as markers and examiners of students' work at all levels as it is of us in our roles as members of appointments and promotions committees, as referees for publication, as reviewers for journals, and as fellow-scholars in our response to and use of work published in our field. And to say that our judgements in these cases are for the most part beyond conclusive demonstration does not, of course, mean that reasons cannot be given and evidence cited to support them: the judgements are, when we are acting up to our own best standards in these matters, far from arbitrary or mere expressions of prejudice. But it means that their rightness cannot be conclusively demonstrated to one who disagrees: we can, ultimately, only say 'Look at this or that or the other aspect – *that* is why it's better, don't you see?', and although the discussion may continue and we may try fresh tactics of persuasion, if the other person does not see, does not *recognize* the qualities in question, then no amount of pointing can force them to do so.

In any given situation, we may of course value one piece of work over another for various pragmatic or instrumental purposes, including those that have led us to be reading it in the first place. Often we are simply in search of information. However, in addition to such purposes, when we read a piece of writing in the humanities, our judgement is very considerably shaped by a dimension of its writing which is not in any straightforward sense to do with what might be called its informational or propositional content, but rather with matters of perspective, of tone, of nuance, of apparent authority, and so on. More specifically still, what we admire and respond to in the best work are certain qualities of noticing and characterizing, certain powers of illuminating and persuading. This can involve merely drawing attention to things previously overlooked or unrecognized, but more often the way in which the noticing or recognizing is expressed, the texture of the characterizing, conveys to the reader something of the flexibility of intelligence or responsiveness of sensibility at work. The angle of entry to the topic, the distribution of emphasis, the implicit placing or comparison, the specific touches by which a world, an episode, a figure, or a book is conjured up and given density or inwardness – all these things convey to us something of the depth of understanding which is present and is, as it were, underwriting any particular statement. This depth of understanding may sometimes be expressed in terms of the overt redirection of our attention it commands; at other times it may seem to depend upon little more than the choice of adverbs by which the description of a person or an action is modified. The forms of expression and kinds of judgement involved are necessarily continuous with, albeit more exact and thoroughly grounded than, those involved in everyday human transactions.

I am not drawing attention to this state of affairs in order either to bewail it or to glory in it. But the undeniable fact of it may help us identify something characteristic of, and perhaps even distinctive about, the humanities. Let me enter two immediate caveats. First, it is of course the case that many things are going on at once in a good piece of scholarly or critical writing, and I am not disputing the significance of the other things. Such work may, for instance, involve drawing upon new knowledge in the narrowest sense (perhaps new manuscript sources or hitherto neglected documents and so on); and nothing I say here is meant to diminish the importance of the basic canons of all intellectual enquiry, such as clarity, exactness, rigour of argument, and so on – those are, it should go without saying, indispensable. There is also the question of an appropriate degree of familiarity with the current state of scholarship in relationship to a particular topic: even the most original scholars do not start from scratch, and the kind of contribution a piece of work makes obviously partly depends on the current state of scholarship on that topic. All of these matters are vital – but they are also, I would suggest, shared by most other forms of intellectual enquiry; they are not in any way distinctive of the humanities.

And that leads to my second caveat. Those working in the natural sciences are also constantly distinguishing good from less good work in their own fields, but, as far as I can tell, attention is focused far more exclusively on the demonstrable validity or otherwise of the work's main contentions, plus concerns about the fruitfulness of the topic and fertility of the methods, rather than on these more elusive matters of tone and perspective. Individual scientists may come to be admired for their creativity or originality, but the meaning and value of their scientific papers does not depend upon the kind of texture of expression

I am pointing to here. In principle, one scientific author could be substituted for another without damaging the truth and importance of the findings the article in question is reporting. The same might be said of some aspects of scholarship in the humanities, but in general the overall cogency of a substantial piece of work seems more closely bound up with the individual voice of its author. This is, interestingly, even true of those critiques which challenge the traditional centrality of 'the human subject': the persuasiveness of any such piece of writing will depend in part upon some highly individual characteristics of the critic's cast of mind and literary skill.

In drawing attention to this aspect of the everyday practice of scholarship in the humanities, it is not the business of ranking one student or scholar as in some sense 'better' than another that is significant, but rather the evidence which reflection on our own experience yields us about the nature of the intellectual activity itself. Such reflection suggests a further implication which may be particularly in need of explicit statement at present: it is simply not true that one can only recognize a piece of work as good of its kind if one happens to agree with its approach or, as we are encouraged to say these days, endorses its methodology. We are all, I suspect, familiar with the opposite experience – namely, recognizing real intellectual quality even though we may not share the approach – and part of the significance of that experience lies in the realization that any particular methodology or theoretical vocabulary only furnishes a set of tools or, at most, a set of lenses; it still takes particular users to make use of them, and they can be made use of more or less skilfully.

For these reasons, the activity of 'characterizing' that is at the heart of such work requires that we become as dexterous as possible in deploying, and in reflecting upon our deployment of, the widest possible range of overlapping vocabularies. An unfortunate effect of much of the recent theoretical self-consciousness in academic disciplines has been to encourage the assumption that any scholar or critic is always working from within a *single* theory or paradigm: one has a favoured approach or methodology, an allegiance to one particular ism, and this, it is claimed, governs the kind of work that can be done. But intellectual practice is not actually like that: focusing on what is conveyed by one manner of expression rather than another draws attention to the fact that such a manner is always under-determined by the particular theoretical model to which allegiance is overtly given. The vocabularies we use in the humanities are in this sense inevitably 'impure': they are amalgams of idioms drawn from more than one intellectual source and from many aspects of everyday expression not explicitly derived from or grounded in any particular theory (which is not to say that they do not rest on or embody assumptions). I am not suggesting here that it is a mark of quality in the humanities to go in for a showy light-footedness or deliberate intellectual magpie-ism, which parades how it has married elements from diverse, and sometimes radically incompatible, sources. I mean, rather, the sense which a piece of writing can give us that, whatever sources of intellectual nourishment have been drawn upon, the results have been digested, absorbed; that there is a controlling understanding which is not reducible to the methodological protocols that have been explicitly announced.

To put it another way, no methodology in the humanities can furnish us with a lexicon and a syntax sufficiently extensive to replace *all* traces of everyday language and idiom. Even the most rebarbative theoretically explicit jargons are shot through with, and embedded in, wider pre-existing vocabularies. The deftness with which this necessary embedding is carried out, the sense of grasp and proportion with which someone makes use of, rather than being made use of by, the terms of a particular approach – these are among the most telling indications of the contrasts between deeper and shallower forms of understanding.

III

One reason for trying to isolate this aspect of the everyday experience of reading work in the humanities is that it seems to offer a way of thinking about not just the distinctiveness but also the value of such work. For, phrases such as 'the quality of noticing and characterizing' or 'the sense of grasp and proportion' refer not to some form of impersonal and inert knowledge, but to the human activity of understanding. Putting it in this way immediately signals a difference of emphasis from the prevailing form of the public discussion of these disciplines. The official language available in the public domain for characterizing the nature of work in the humanities at present often seems to reduce to the formula: 'skills + information = knowledge'. If that were really an adequate formula, then the model of good work would have to be something like the encyclopedia entry. Such compilations have their merits and their uses, and they do indeed call upon important skills – the ability to be both clear and concise, to give an orderly exposition of a complex topic, and so on. But compared to a brilliantly imaginative piece of historical reconstruction or an illuminatingly perceptive piece of criticism, the encyclopedia entry is for the most part flat and inert, a mere vehicle, not an actual journey. It tends precisely to be a summary of collective knowledge, not an expression of individual understanding. And it tends to use adverbs very sparsely indeed, including adverbs such as 'sparsely'.

If we have to use formulae – and it is a predictable part of my case that something has gone wrong if we do find ourselves conducting the discussion in terms of formulae – then it would surely be something more like: 'experience + reflection = understanding'. It is vital, as I suggested earlier, to emphasize that the goal of work in the humanities, in particular, is better described as 'understanding' than as 'knowledge'. One of the consequences of insisting on that distinction is the recognition that whereas knowledge is seen as in some sense objective, 'out there', a pile or hoard that exists whether anyone is tending it or not and which any suitably energetic person can climb to the top of, understanding is a human activity that depends in part upon the qualities of the understander.

Several things follow from this. One, which has practical consequences for our notions of assessment, is that the prevailing conception of 'research', understood as the discovery of new knowledge, cannot be applied in these disciplines as readily as in the natural and social sciences. I have tried to make this case more than once before (see the essay 'Against Prodspeak: "Research" in the Humanities', in my *English Pasts*) and shall not rehearse it again here, but it has another implication which bears upon the present theme: namely, that whereas in the sciences it seems that the three assessment categories of 'research', 'teaching', and 'public or professional work' can be treated as three quite distinct activities, this is much less true in the humanities. To a working scientist, there is an obvious and readily identifiable distinction between discovering new knowledge and communicating old knowledge. Research is the former, teaching or writing for a lay public are essentially the latter, and one can therefore see a certain brusque administrative logic in attempting to assess and fund these activities in different ways. But that framework serves the humanities much less well. If I write an essay for a scholarly collection on a topic where I have been reading a good deal in what we sometimes call the primary texts, and then I give a lecture to a non-specialist but still highly educated and sophisticated audience about some aspect of this same topic, and then I write a review-essay for, say, the *Times Literary Supplement* discussing some recent publications in this field, and finally I prepare a third-year undergraduate class on one of the primary texts – in this continuum of my activities as a scholar it is much less clear where 'research' begins and ends. I know that my own thinking and writing have been at least as deeply influenced by certain brilliant review-essays I have read in such publications as the *London Review of Books* or the *New York Review of Books* as they have by reading items which assessment procedures more easily recognize as 'research publications', and the same is true for many colleagues. This may tell us something about the nature and importance of the whole spectrum of our scholarly or intellectual activities in their bearing upon that more limited form of writing which is now taken as the exclusive index of 'research'.

A further practical implication of this line of argument is that at all levels the model of assessment in the humanities has to be judgement not measurement, and judgement cannot, without loss and distortion, be rendered in quantitative terms nor can its grounds ever be made wholly 'transparent' (to use another of the current Edspeak buzzwords). This last suggestion can seem particularly unpalatable when viewed from the perspective of those who are judged adversely: the student whose work has been failed, the colleague who has unsuccessfully applied for promotion, the department which has been ranked lower than it expected in the scramble for funds, and so on. Again, I would emphasize that of course reasons must be given for such judgements, and I am not in the least defending a policy of closed doors or any other procedure that can make it easier for mere prejudice to get its way unchallenged. My point is simply that the process of justifying the judgement inevitably involves an infinite regress: no amount of spelling out of the criteria and laying down of procedures can spirit away the ineliminable element of judgement, and that judgement cannot be made conclusively demonstrable to anyone who does not at least partly recognize the persuasiveness of the more local identifications on which it rests.

It may be better, even at the risk of initial public misunderstanding, to acknowledge that this is a proper reflection of the nature of what is most valuable to us about good work in the humanities rather than trying to pretend otherwise. One of the most satisfying aspects of a crossword puzzle or a chess problem or some elementary arithmetic questions is that you can achieve a kind of closure: you can not only find the one right answer but you can know that you have done so. Very little about work in the humanities is like that. We search for patterns in the carpet, but we are aware that the characterization of any one pattern can never be conclusive. As I have already suggested, everything we say in these subjects is challengeable, not just in the sense in which knowledge in the sciences is challengeable by bringing in new information or revealing flaws in the logic of the original reasoning, but challengeable by bringing to bear another idiom, another context, another emphasis, another perspective, another sensibility. And these are always matters of judgement, albeit of disciplined and experienced judgement rather than merely subjective or arbitrary judgement. The greater persuasiveness of the new account cannot be demonstrated conclusively: it can only attempt to plug itself into our understanding at a greater number of points, to build more plausibility and more illumination into a rearrangement of what is already in some sense partly known.

This means that, as scholars in the humanities, we should not be willing to re-describe what we most value about what we do purely in terms either of 'skills' or of 'new findings'. Deciding whether or in what way the character of Dorothea Brooke in *Middlemarch* is self-deceived may be central to our understanding and estimation of that novel, but it is not a process that can be reduced to the exercise of 'skills'. Similarly, exploring what it might mean to say that Nietzsche's critique of morality is flawed by his not wholly ironic self-dramatization – a knotty, disputable, but perhaps profound comment on that brilliant and exasperating writer – cannot very easily be represented as pushing back the frontiers of knowledge by means of 'research'. It is possible that Thomas Mann already had a deeper grasp of this question a century ago than that displayed in the latest academic monograph on Nietzsche, yet we could hardly say that this just means the 'research' has already been 'done' and we merely have to look up the 'results'. It may mean that in brooding on this question a modern scholar will make at least as much progress with the matter as a result of re-reading a bit of Thomas Mann as by mopping up all the recent articles identified in an online literature search, but, as Alexander Nehamas's marvellous *Nietzsche: Life as Literature* showed some years ago, there can be no recipe for doing good new work on such a topic. Better thinking in the humanities often occurs as a result of a sufficiently thoughtful and responsive re-encounter with the ideas of figures long dead, including figures who did not belong to the same discipline, or indeed to any discipline.

A further consequence of this argument is that the most fertile conditions for stimulating good work in the humanities may have more to do with the range and qualities of the minds an individual scholar engages with and learns from than it does with the concentration of expertise, in its narrow form, in a given sub-field. This, too, has implications for the funding of research, since it seems that in some branches of science and medicine it can make sense to arrange funding so as to concentrate researchers on certain topics exclusively in a very small number of institutions. This comparison again draws attention to the ways in which 'research' may be a dangerously misleading model for the humanities. Far from being beneficial, it would be intellectually damaging not just to teaching but also to scholarship in the respective fields were, say, all modern German history PhDs to be done at Cambridge, or all eighteenth-century English poetry PhDs at Leeds, and so on. Such concentration may reduce rather than enhance the likelihood of stimulating contact, both for scholars in these sub-fields and for the larger scholarly communities from which they are thereby withdrawn. Though there can sometimes be benefits from undertaking collaborative projects, as well as economies of scale in practical terms, it remains true that in the humanities the basic unit of funding has to be the individual, whether established scholar or new graduate student, and it is not wholly predictable where any particular such individual will most flourish.

Although my focus here is not on pedagogical practice, this argument does also have consequences for how we talk about teaching. For example, it suggests that we do better to acknowledge, rather than seek to disguise, the extent to which, beyond a minimum introductory level, education in the humanities largely consists in a form of apprenticeship. At each stage, in the form relevant to that stage, the student is exposed to contact with someone who carries on the trade at a high level, and is thereby encouraged to develop an autonomous capacity for noticing and characterizing. Much of this can undoubtedly be learned, but only to a limited degree can it be taught; there is at least some truth in the old adage that it is more readily caught than taught. In this respect, much teaching in the humanities partakes of the central activity of literary criticism, where the critic points to features of the work in question and says 'See?' Of course, what is to be seen, and why it may be important to see it, can be spelled out and justified; but the extent to which the student comes to 'see' it for herself will largely depend on the human qualities of expressiveness and subtlety in the teacher and on the responsiveness and curiosity of the student. We should not accept that 'study skills', abstracted from learning about a particular topic, can, to any great extent, substitute for this engagement. Introducing students to the study of the humanities is more akin to inciting them to take part in a discussion than it is to equipping them to process information efficiently.

It is important to recognize that all metaphors about 'joining a discussion' or being 'dexterous in one's deployment of an idiom' can appear both self-satisfied and coercive to those who, setting out from quite other linguistic or cultural starting-points, fear that a lack of facility with one peculiar way of going on may simply operate as a means to exclude them. Such reminders are legitimate checks on any tendency we may have to take particular contingent conditions for granted. But it should be clear that my aim in this chapter is not to engage with those reminders in any extended way, but rather to urge us not to be thrown so far on to the defensive by them or by other challenges that we mis-describe what we actually do and actually value. Learning how to understand and characterize human actions and expressions across time and culture does not presuppose the validity of currently favoured starting-points. On the contrary, one of the features that distinguishes some of the most original work in these fields is a persuasive case for the benefits of starting from somewhere else. Discussions can be interrupted and redirected, and a different voice may be particularly effective in disturbing the existing participants into re-examining matters they had come to take for granted.

At present, one particularly favoured self-description in what tend, in this context, to be referred to as 'the human sciences' is the contention that the distinguishing operation in these disciplines is 'critique'. Critique always aims to challenge the givenness of any starting-point, assumption, or range of reference, and usually to unmask the potentially sinister interests that are served by allowing any such starting-point to go unchallenged. For certain purposes, this can, needless to say, be a wholly fruitful, indeed necessary, strategy to pursue. But at the level of concrete instances, good work, like good talk or any other form of worthwhile human relationship, *depends upon* being able to assume an extended shared world. This is not necessarily sinister or exclusive, nor is it necessarily to be equated, as it too often is in glib forms of ideology-critique, with particular social groups or interests. People can learn about new worlds starting from many different backgrounds. As a result, individuals will frequently turn out to have far more in common as a basis from which to engage in an intellectual exchange about a specific book or episode than the prior statements of their 'methodological position' or 'social identity' might suggest. The model of critique presents itself as insurgent because of its insistence on the social locatedness of all arguments. However, the effect of this is constantly to move discussion to a transcendental standpoint from which the necessary limits of any particular exchanges can be identified. This has its point in philosophical enquiry, but a too-swift move to a meta-theoretical standpoint tends to obstruct or deaden discussion of the texture of individual instances, and therefore cannot be a prescription for *all* work in the humanities. Similarly, if there is a sense in which we can speak, metaphorically, of individuals talking different 'languages', then the ideal should surely be to facilitate the richest, most nuanced exchange about particular matters, which requires language-learning and translation, not the reduction of these languages into a lowest common denominator or a kind of intellectual equivalent of Esperanto.

Furthermore, insofar as the emphasis on critique does proceed to engage with concrete instances, its tendency towards what has been termed 'the hermeneutics of suspicion' can have a limiting as well as enabling power. In much work done under this inspiration, there is a curious asymmetry in which the assumptions of the figures who are the objects of study are subjected to a much more severe regime than are the assumptions of the ones doing the studying. My recipe would be the opposite: extend the greatest possible imaginative sympathy to the expressions of the human agents we study, but combine it with the greatest possible scepticism about any of the explanatory mechanisms by means of which we try to account for their actions. Depth of understanding involves something which is more than merely a matter of deconstructive alertness; it involves a measure of interpretative charity and at least the beginnings of a wide responsiveness. Since the processes of identification, sympathy, imagination, and so on can suggest an undisciplined subjectivism, some of the severer methodological protocols that have been fashionable in the humanities in recent decades have sought to outlaw them. But in reality they are essential to the amplest forms of understanding, whether in scholarly work or other aspects of human experience. If we were to treat all our interlocutors' utterances merely as symptomatic rather than as expressive or communicative, we would soon find ourselves leading affectively thin and relentlessly diagnostic lives. It is true that the critic or historian does not, and should not, take at face value all statements by the individuals they are studying, and it is also true that scholars may sometimes bring to the interpretation of such statements concepts which the agents themselves did not possess. But understanding them *as* human expressions, with meanings that belonged to a world that is not identical to our world, is the indispensable starting-point, and that requires a form of human sympathy at least as much as it does narrow-eyed suspicion. Without an element of such interpretive charity, there will always be a considerable misdirection of forensic energy if we confine ourselves to attempting to secure a conviction against such utterances on the grounds of the unacceptable attitudes they inadvertently betray or disclose.

IV

In conclusion, a brief comment on the question of justification or defence, beginning with a very general point already touched on, namely that justification involves some kind of appeal to shared values. Alert practical critics will notice that in this book I make liberal use of such adverbs as 'surely': that is one of the rhetorical markers precisely of this kind of appeal to pre-existing, if not always articulated, common experience (as is the use, also deliberately prominent, of the first-person plural). The core of the argument here is simply stated. A society in which individuals never attempted to identify and refine their experiences of other individuals in whom they partly recognized themselves would also be one which could never be persuaded of the point of studying the humanities. In practice, the persuasiveness of argument will always depend upon this prior potential for recognition. But recognition grows out of particulars: it cannot be lodged in the mind by concepts alone.

Thus, there will be situations in which the best tactic for defending the humanities in the face of real or simulated scepticism may be to say: 'See, this is what we do: terrific, isn't it?' If the response from the sober-suited self-styled administrative realists around the table is to say that they don't see that it's terrific at all, it may, paradoxically, be better to let the discussion degenerate into a version of the pantomime exchange 'Oh yes it is/Oh no it isn't', rather than to try to re-describe the value of the activity in terms drawn from a different, instrumental world of discourse. In practice, of course, discussion will not tend to follow this pattern, at least not in its pure form, but imagining the logic of such an exchange can be a helpful heuristic, a way of reminding ourselves what realities, in terms of concrete achievement, lie behind the familiar appeal to bland abstractions. And while speaking of particulars, we should register the subliminal capacity of the phrase 'concrete achievement' to summon up disconcertingly apt images: there is something both pleasing and telling about the fantasy of responding to official requests to 'justify' the humanities by having a series of dumper trucks deposit a huge pile of excellent scholarly books on the steps of the relevant ministry.

Put more soberly, the point here is that the effectiveness of any response that we can make when faced with a (potentially unsympathetic) request to characterize and justify the humanities may be as much a matter of tone and confidence as it is of definitions and arguments. The humanities, it has been well said, 'explore what it means to be human: the words, ideas, narratives and the art and artefacts that help us make sense of our lives and the world we live in; how we have created it and are created by it'. The forms of enquiry grouped together under this label are ways of encountering the record of human activity in its greatest richness and diversity. To attempt to deepen our understanding of this or that aspect of that activity is an intelligible and purposeful expression of disciplined human curiosity and is – insofar as the phrase makes any sense in this context – an end in itself. It should be clear that I intend these deliberately intransigent remarks to be the opposite of a counsel of despair. Very little that is of any interest or significance in our lives is like a crossword puzzle or a chess problem. The kinds of understanding and judgement exercised in the humanities are of a piece with the kinds of understanding and judgement involved in living a life. All we can say at this point is that *that*, in the end, is why they interest us and seem worthwhile, and we must then recognize that we have reached a point beyond which justification cannot go. In trying to 'justify' the humanities, as in trying to live a life, what may turn out to matter most is holding one's nerve.

5

The Highest Aspirations and Ideals: Universities as a Public Good

I

Almost a century ago, the American social critic Thorstein Veblen published a book entitled *The Higher Learning in America: A Memorandum on the Conduct of Universities by Businessmen*, in which he declared: 'In a general way, the place of the university in the culture of Christendom is still substantially the same as it has been from the beginning. Ideally, and in the popular apprehension, it is, as it has always been, a corporation for the cultivation and care of the community's highest aspirations and ideals.' Given that Veblen's larger purpose, as indicated by his book's subtitle, involved a vigorous critique of current tendencies in American higher education, the confidence and downrightness of this declaration are very striking. We, of course, are not now inclined to speak of 'Christendom', though the term may serve as a reminder of the roots of the university and even of part of its character well into the nineteenth century. Veblen's language hints that some of this spiritual legacy may still be at work in modern conceptions, since a community's 'highest aspirations and ideals' may seem to go beyond the usual understanding of even the activities of education and research. Moreover, the suggestion is that the 'cultivation and care' of these ideals entails a certain kind of withdrawal from society's everyday activities, an indication of a concern with considerations that are longer term and less material. And I particularly like Veblen's passing insistence that this elevated conception of the university and the 'popular apprehension' of it coincide, about which he was surely right. Even today, after all the vast changes that have overtaken universities and that separate them from the institutions that Veblen knew, and despite – as much as because of – the great educational enfranchisement that has taken place in recent decades, there still lingers this popular conception, almost a longing, that the university should be a protected space in which thoughts and ideas of this kind can be pursued to the highest level. Whatever the reality of the experience of actually attending one of today's semi-marketized, employment-oriented institutions, there remains a strong popular desire that they should, at their best, incarnate a set of 'aspirations and ideals' that go beyond any form of economic return.

It is crucial that attempts to make the case for universities in present circumstances should not lose sight of this deep and pervasive conviction. For there is, as I have already suggested, an inescapable difficulty involved in any argument that looks like an attempt to justify something. Inevitably, a certain aura of defensiveness hangs about such exercises. The initial presumption seems to be that the value or point of the thing is in question and needs to be defended to a doubting or unsympathetic audience. If enough voices ask insistently enough what the 'point' of something is, that usually indicates the prevalence of some scepticism or, at the very least, uncertainty about its value, shading over in some cases to outright hostility. Those who attempt to 'speak up' for universities in the present nearly always seem, in this way, to start on the back foot.

The problem is in one respect obvious. Justification is called for in the first place when the point or value of some activity cannot be treated as self-evident, where there exists some imagined audience who are going to take some persuading. It is, of course, a general truth about justification that it can, by its very nature, only succeed when the values being appealed to are already partly shared among the audience to whom the justification is addressed. But if that audience seems to give priority to a set of values ostensibly unsympathetic to the cause in question, there will always be a temptation to try to couch the justification in terms which are thought to have the greatest appeal, even if that ends up mis-describing what one is trying to justify. In this way, champions of the universities find themselves saying, in effect: 'We realize that we may seem irrelevant or self-indulgent, but actually we contribute to economic growth more than you might think.'

It does not seem to me that those who speak for or about universities need to adopt this defensive posture. In saying this I am certainly not forgetting or underestimating the degree of misunderstanding and hostility that universities in Britain, at least, have encountered from some politicians and some sections of the media over the past two or three decades. But I suspect that among the public at large there is, potentially, a much greater reservoir of interest in, and potential appreciation of, the work of universities than this narrow and defensive official discourse ever succeeds in tapping into. In talking to audiences outside universities (some of whom may these days be graduates, of course) I am struck by the level of curiosity about, and enthusiasm for, ideas and the quest for greater understanding, whether in history and literature, or physics and biology, or any number of other fields. Some members of these audiences may not have had the chance to study these things themselves, but they very much want their children to have the opportunity to do so; others may have enjoyed only limited and perhaps not altogether happy experiences of higher education in their own lives, but have now in their adulthood discovered a keen amateur reading interest in these subjects; others still may have retired from occupations which largely frustrated their intellectual or aesthetic inclinations and are now hungry for stimulation. Such audiences do not want to be told that we judge the success of a university education by how much more graduates can earn than non-graduates, any more than they want to hear how much scholarship and science may indirectly contribute to GDP. They are, rather, susceptible to the romance of ideas and the power of beauty; they want to learn about far-off times and far-away worlds; they expect to hear language used more inventively, more exactly, more evocatively than it normally is in their workaday world; they want to know that, somewhere, human understanding is being pressed to its limits, unconstrained by immediate practical outcomes. These audiences are not all of one mind, needless to say, and not all sections of society are equally well represented among these audiences. At various points in their lives they may have other priorities, and there will always be competing demands on their interests and sympathies. But it is notice-able, and surely regrettable, how little the public discourse about universities in contemporary society makes any kind of appeal to this widespread appreciation on the part of ordinary intelligent citizens that there should be places where these kinds of enquiries are being pursued at their highest level. Part of the problem may be that while universities are spectacularly good at producing new forms of under-standing, they are not always very good at explaining what they are doing when they do this.

Instead of defensively anticipating a hostile and reductively instru-mental disdain for universities, it may, as I have already suggested, be better to begin by considering, in an analytical yet also positive man-ner, what kinds of things are distinctive about universities, compared to various superficially cognate institutions, and what they, at their best, do that we would not wish to be without. This is not, I believe, the same thing as falling into the empty boosterism of annual reports or pressure-group lobbying. We ought to acknowledge that, in practice, contemporary universities do not perform some of their distinctive tasks all that well. Not to acknowledge this would be, yet again, to underestimate the intelligence of the public who are well aware that all is not well with many of our overcrowded, over-regulated institutions of higher education.

But even if we do not fall into the trap of defensiveness, there is still a difficulty – a literary or expository difficulty above all – in making a case in terms of widely shared values. The danger is of ending up with little more than a parade of abstract nouns. One only needs to think of the empty, portentous prose of that representative genre of our time, the 'mission statement'. The message of most of these dreary documents can be summarized as 'We aim to achieve whatever gen-eral goals are currently approved of.' Justificatory statements about universities have a fatal tendency to fall into this kind of corporate boiler-plate, with traditional phrases about 'the pursuit of truth' or 'the cultivation of the mind' now being jostled aside by more recently minted clichés about 'contributing to the knowledge-economy' or 'fostering diversity, respect, and inclusiveness', and so on.

It is difficult to give a general description of an activity in terms which are at once lively and specific, and it is particularly hard to characterize what is valuable about the life of the mind in ways that go beyond such familiar formulae. For this reason, it seems to me that champions of universities may do better to operate in modes that are more tactical, opportunist, and polemical, engaging with particular proposals or debates rather than attempting to come up with some all-embracing general formulation from scratch. Criticism can, needless to say, appear to be 'merely negative', but in reality good criticism is bound to be drawing upon ideals and values by whose lights the claim or measure under scrutiny falls short, and in so doing a positive picture is allowed to emerge without having to strut about in the full regalia of abstraction. In addition, criticism can legitimately enlist humour in its cause: making readers laugh at something can be a good way to engage their sympathies, as well as making it more likely they will keep reading. The chapters in Part Two of this book are occasional pieces in just this sense – responses, provoked by a particular measure or moment in the recent history of universities, but responses which attempt at least to begin the task of making a better idiom available in which to carry on the discussion.

We should also recognize that some of the difficulties encountered in making the case for universities derive from a wider climate of unanalysed pseudo-relativism (I say 'unanalysed' because such a position, when made explicit, invariably turns out to be internally inconsistent as well as unliveable). An egalitarian ethos which may be laudable in itself can generate that kind of 'who's to say?' or 'that's just your opinion' posture which implicitly denies the possibility of reasoned arguments for some things being more worthwhile than others. And in a climate where so much of the discussion of universities turns on questions of funding, it has come to seem almost inevitable that the only criterion for the expenditure of 'public money' assumed to command widespread acceptance where this ethos prevails is the consumerist one of increased prosperity. (We should, incidentally, not let the familiar distinction between 'public' and 'private' money pass unchallenged, especially given the extent to which so-called 'private finance' is in practice also sustained by 'public' infrastructure and subsidy.) This all too easily translates into the economistic philistinism of insisting that the activities carried on in universities need to be justified, perhaps can *only* be justified, by demonstrating their contribution to the economy. In the face of this, one has to make, over and over again, the obvious point that a society does not educate the next generation in order for them to contribute to its economy. It educates them in order that they should extend and deepen their understanding of themselves and the world, acquiring, in the course of this form of growing up, kinds of knowledge and skill which will be useful in their eventual employment, but which will no more be the sum of their education than that employment will be the sum of their lives. And this general point about education takes a particular form in universities, where, whatever level of professional or vocational 'training' is also undertaken, the governing purpose involves extending human understanding through open-ended enquiry. From wholly laudable motives, we constantly fall into the trap of justifying an activity – one initially (and perhaps for long thereafter) undertaken because of its intrinsic interest and worth – as something which we do because it yields incidental benefits which are popular with those not in a position to appreciate the activity's intrinsic interest and worth. If we find ourselves saying that what is valuable about learning to play the violin well is that it helps us develop the manual dexterity that will be useful for typing, then we are stuck in a traffic-jam of carts in front of horses.

Universities are, it should be recognized, a problem for governments, and they are an especial problem for populist governments in market democracies. The only two forms of justification that such governments assume will be accepted by their electorates are first, manpower planning, the training of future employees in a particular economy; and second, certain narrowly defined benefits of 'research', especially the medical, technological, and economic benefits. A third function, the preservation, cultivation, and transmission of a cultural tradition, cuts some ice if it is understood to be confined to a small number of outstanding institutions, somewhat analogous to the case for national galleries and museums. A fourth justification, one that has had considerable purchase in the United States and, in a different idiom, in France, concerns socialization in civic values, but that has never played very well in Britain, partly because the implicit nature of the political and social ideals allegedly governing British life have not, to most people, seemed to need explicit formulation and inculcation. That complacent view has been considerably shaken in recent years, and official recognition of the needs of an increasingly heterogeneous population suggests this justification will become more and more prominent in the future. It is also noticeable that universities are increasingly being expected to be instruments of 'social mobility', as society's bad conscience about entrenched inequalities seeks solace from misleading metaphors about 'level playing-fields' that allow it to pretend that expanded recruitment to higher education can be a substitute for real structural change to the distribution of wealth in society.

Governments select from among their portfolio of justifications depending on occasion and audience: when boasting of the standing of Britain's 'top' universities among the world elite, they laud 'research excellence'; when speaking for 'UK plc' they insist on 'training for employment' and 'technology transfer'; when speaking directly to the electorate they emphasize 'opportunity' and 'the development of talent'. The catchphrases change with social and political fashion, but the underlying tensions between these various purposes remain recognizable. And, as I suggested earlier, various justifications do not simply differ among themselves; in some forms they can be in active contradiction with each other. Thus, from the nineteenth century onwards, the research ideal has obviously been somewhat at odds with that of character-formation: the narrowness of focus required by the former tends to militate against the breadth and diversity conducive to the latter. Similarly, the currently fashionable emphasis on enabling people to develop their potential is equally at odds with the no less fashionable emphasis on fostering economic competitiveness: what if the potential that people find they have to develop is to become unsaleably esoteric poets?

Throughout their long history, universities have been selective institutions: at different times selective by religious, vocational, or political criteria, nearly always selective in terms of social class, and in the course of the twentieth century increasingly selective by intellectual aptitude. The surface egalitarianism of market democracies is uneasy with claims about the differential capacities of individuals and still more with ideas about intrinsic differences of worth between activities. The ideology of consumer choice is that all wants are in principle equal: the only acceptable indication of value is consumer demand. Anything else smacks of 'elitism', the paternalist attempt by some to dictate to others what they ought to want. The idea that some things are intrinsically more valuable than others and that they can be seriously cultivated only by those with the relevant aptitudes raises hackles.

That is particularly the case when there is any suspicion that the selection in question has been influenced by traditional forms of privilege. To bring out what is at issue here, it is interesting to consider, by contrast, the nearly complete absence of anxieties about 'elitism' where the upper rungs of major sports are concerned (and something similar might be said about conservatoires of music and dance). There is widespread acceptance of the principle of utterly ruthless selection by ability, both at the level of sports academies and youth squads, and at the level of top teams competing internationally, as well as acceptance that those who succeed at these levels should have the best facilities and back-up that money can buy, including, in some cases, taxpayers' money. One obvious pre-condition for this public support is the perception that neither social class nor, increasingly, ethnic origin constitute any kind of barrier to success in these sports. When there have remained misgivings on this score, as there were until relatively recently with sports such as cricket and rugby union, charges of 'elitism' quickly come into play. It is also essential that the sports should have wide popular appeal and be at least in part financed by a paying public, who in turn expect high standards of performance. In these circumstances, individuals from ordinary backgrounds who excel at activities for which there is widespread popular enthusiasm are not automatically suspected of being 'superior', and rigorous selection by aptitude is seen as being both essential and fair. Universities do not enjoy these advantages.

So, the fundamental conundrum facing those attempting to justify public support for universities is this: much of what goes on in them is, by its very nature, likely to be regarded as both 'useless' and 'elitist', that is to say, it is hard to justify in terms either of its direct contribution to economic prosperity or of its direct contribution to 'social inclusiveness'. But here we may start to bump up against the limits of what it will prove fruitful to try to argue in public discussion of universities. As I emphasize throughout this book, it is difficult for politicians in a market democracy such as ours to find a language in which to promote the claims of things which have traditionally been regarded as 'good in themselves' as against the claims of what 'consumers' are said to 'want'. Universities serve various instrumental purposes, as they always have done, but at the same time they centrally involve activities whose justification goes beyond instrumental purposes. Finding a language in which to talk about this ineliminable tension is certainly not easy, but if we do not try, then the critics will be right to say that we have let the case for universities go by default. In some moods we may feel that the most we can realistically hope for, in the words of a great master both of realism and of repetition, is to 'fail again, fail better'. Even so, we must try again.

II

Those who work in universities are frequently told that it is imperative to be 'realistic' in making the case for these institutions, and that unless the case is made in terms which governments and taxpayers recognize, we risk 'shooting ourselves in the foot'. But what this involves, at least in part, is employing categories and descriptions which we know, or ought to know, misrepresent the true purpose and value of much of what is done in universities. And this is one source of the malaise that now afflicts so many academics in countries such as Britain. They feel obliged to speak an alien language. They are constantly having to cobble together statements which purport to demonstrate the contribution their disciplines make to the national economy or other extraneous goals when they know in their heart of hearts that these are not the purpose of their activities and are not what made these disciplines interesting or valuable to them or others in the first place. Similarly, they feel obliged to undertake, and to publish the results of, their research according to a timetable and a template drawn up in accordance with regulatory criteria. It is hardly surprising if many of their public comments lapse into complaint or, worse still, special pleading, and this risks forfeiting some of the public support which might otherwise be drawn upon.

Official representatives of higher education no doubt employ the required language in good faith, and they presumably feel confident that their own understanding of the character of intellectual enquiry is not affected by their pragmatic recognition of the necessity of using that language. But there is a double risk here. First, if that is the only type of argument put forward by the champions of universities, then quite soon only the activities which seem to deliver in those terms will be judged worthy of support. And second, the result of such a monochromatic discourse is that we all become inured to these phrases and start not to notice how they colonize our minds. When we read, for the hundredth time, that scientific research should be supported because it contributes to 'growth', it sounds like the ritual incantation of a truism, and we cease even to notice the way it represents intellectual enquiry as though it were a kind of hormone and 'growth' some kind of unambiguous good. We scarcely register when we are told, as we repeatedly are, that universities contribute to our 'national competitiveness' what a skewed and perhaps even undesirable goal this would be. One of the salutary effects of returning from this world of public discourse to the studies which universities actually promote is to be jolted out of this kind of numbed acquiescence and reminded that words are our masters as well as our servants.

In this connection, it would be interesting to submit the speeches and articles about universities by politicians, academic administrators, business leaders and others to a small textual experiment. We could try removing all references to 'economic prosperity', 'growth', 'our economic competitiveness', 'wealth creation', and so on, and then consider whether there is anything left which looks at all like an argument in favour of the value of universities and the activities they pursue. I suspect the resulting texts would resemble those pictures of pre-modern battlefields where small clumps of survivors are left going through the motions of military activity though they have lost contact with the main army and will be fatally vulnerable to the first concerted attack by the enemy. A few nominal values will be left wandering through the scarred and vacant landscapes of these denuded paragraphs – this one with the once-proud title 'culture' still legible on its shrivelled pennant, that one left dragging a limber marked 'excellence' to which no piece of artillery is now attached – but they have no fight left in them and no sense of their place in a larger strategy.

Mythical creatures tell us a lot about a society's hopes and fears: they are often a way of externalizing and giving dramatic force to desires and anxieties that are in some way resistant to frank acknowledgement. The mythical beast that haunts this particular discussion is 'the taxpayer'. This morose, prickly creature is intensely suspicious of all contact with others, fearing the abduction and loss of its hoard, the fruits of what it likes to call its 'labours' (such fruits are always 'hard-earned'). Actually, it's surprising that this beast has any time in which to labour, since it is always represented as devoting itself to the scrutiny of what various predators threaten to do with its possessions, itself ever ready to pounce at the slightest suggestion that they might be being shared with other animals. But in the great poetic narratives in which we encounter this mythical creature, it is also represented as easily distracted or placated: if it is told that some part of its hoard will be used to create bigger hoards for all creatures, including itself, then it becomes surprisingly tame and compliant. Protecting and enlarging its hoard seems to be its only activity: it is as monocultural as the ant, but far less cooperative and resourceful. Were it an actual rather than mythical creature, these limiting and self-frustrating characteristics would surely soon lead it to become extinct.

It is significant, I think, that the pitch which universities make to their alumni when hoping to solicit donations from them is different from that which they make when notionally addressing government and 'the taxpayer'. Alumni are assumed to be susceptible to the appeal of intellectual achievement and creative power. They are treated as though they would be proud to help support a brilliant new interpretation of *The Odyssey* or a fertile hypothesis about the behaviour of unimaginably distant galaxies, without having to be persuaded that these also contribute to increased sales of widgets. In fact, they immediately see that this latter move is phoney and irrelevant, partly because they may well have made their money in selling widgets and so they know that undertaking these scholarly enquiries would be an absurdly roundabout way to improve the manufacture and marketing of such objects, and partly because they precisely want to support something that they feel has more intrinsic and lasting value than that sort of commercial or financial activity. Moreover, most donors realize that it is not for them to try to micro-manage what a university does with their money: they may have chosen to support a particular field at a particular university not just because they have some independent interest in it, but because they believe that it represents a concentration of unusually talented people who will make much better judgements about how to advance and teach their field than the donors themselves could. And finally, donors are allowed to be guided by the same range of emotions and inclinations, including gratitude and generosity, and by the same mixture of sentimental attachments and sheer longing as the rest of us, rather than being assumed to operate as rational robots exclusively concerned to maximize economic prosperity.

Reliance on overly individualistic and economistic premises repeatedly drives public discussion of universities up various kinds of blind alleys. Thus, it is sometimes argued that there is no reason why those who do not themselves go to university should contribute, through their taxes, to the costs of those who do. But this is to treat a university education and whatever flows from it as a purely private good. I may choose not to have children, but I am happy to contribute to the costs of maternity hospitals, primary schools, and so on because I want to live in a society that makes civilized provision for these things. I may rarely or never visit various kinds of specialized museums since I am not particularly interested in their contents, but I am happy to contribute to their costs through taxation because I want to live in a society which cares for these things, which does not forget its past, and which recognizes the imaginative and emotional stimulus such objects can provide. There are a great number of forms of public provision of which I may not be a direct beneficiary but which I believe society collectively should attempt to support, and I suspect that this conviction is shared very widely indeed, or would be were the case clearly made. Obviously, each of these forms of public provision has its own features and may require, in particular political contexts, its own supporting arguments. I am not suggesting that the various activities mentioned here are in all respects comparable to those of teaching and studying in a university. But I am suggesting that we do already, in all kinds of ways, recognize the claims on us of public goods, from defence through health and welfare to education and culture, and so elaborating and extending the logic of these claims is one potentially fruitful way to advance understanding of, and support for, the character of universities. The spirit of the argument, whatever its details, surely has to point towards the conviction memorably expressed long ago by the second President of the United States, John Adams: 'The whole people must take upon themselves the education of the whole people, and must be willing to bear the expense of it.'

In articulating the argument for education as a public good, we must be careful not to overstate the case. There is a tendency among champions of higher education to make universities not just compatible with almost all currently approved moral and political values but the necessary, and even at times the sufficient, means of their realization. For example, in _Not for Profit: Why Democracy Needs the Humanities_ Martha Nussbaum comes perilously close to appearing to suggest that respect for, and tolerance of, other people is only likely to be achieved by those who have taken some kind of 'great books' course at college. We may certainly hope that in helping to expand people's cultural awareness we are not narrowing their human sympathies, but there may be no necessary connection in either direction. Almost all arguments that seem to suggest that scholarship, science, or culture turn their practitioners into 'better people' are awkwardly vulnerable to obvious counter-examples. The disciplined free play of the mind over a given topic that is at the heart of scholarly and scientific enquiry is principally a cognitive achievement, not a moral one, at least not directly. The fact that someone can make a dazzling breakthrough in the understanding of nature while at the same time behaving abominably in other aspects of life and holding deplorable political views is not an argument against the value of scientific enquiry. Something similar has to be acknowledged about the humanities, even if we feel that the tension in that case between the kind of understanding required for the scholarly achievement and the apparent lack of understanding displayed by the abominable behaviour may sometimes be rather more marked.

The discussions in Britain in the autumn of 2010 surrounding the Browne Report on university funding underlined more emphatically than ever the need to make the case for higher education as a public as well as a private good (see Chapter 10, below). This is important to a proper understanding of universities, but also important tactically in marshalling support for them. As I indicated earlier, it is a mistake to see this as a sectional cause, merely protecting the interests of the present generation of students (together perhaps with university teachers): it has to be presented as a general social cause which all citizens can support regardless of whether they or their children happen to be at university at the moment. But – and this is the great difficulty of attempting to make this case in the national media – it is crucial that this social good should not be reduced to a purely economic good. Even if it is allowed that there might be some non-material benefits from education for the *individual* – in terms, perhaps, of self-fulfilment or enhanced intellectual capacity – there is still a tendency to confine any possible *social* good to the usual litany about 'productivity', 'competitiveness', 'innovation', and 'growth'. The discourse tends to be structured so that the non-economic is equated with the private, the economic with the public. Instead of this, we need to show that there is a public, not merely private, benefit from higher education that can be characterized in various, not merely economic, terms.

This is most urgent in respect of the humanities. As I mentioned earlier, there is in place a public conviction that science leads to discoveries, inventions, and applications that directly improve human welfare (though this connection is far from obvious with a few of the more rarefied fields such as pure mathematics or astrophysics). This conviction, whatever its tensions or contradictions, makes the justification of the place of the scientific disciplines easier, and that in turn tends to mean that they are more successful in making their case when it comes to matters such as increased funding. But, as I argued in the previous chapter, the 'point' or utility of the humanities cannot be so readily summarized or immediately grasped. The relevant official or professional bodies, such as the Arts and Humanities Research Council or the British Academy, have produced hefty documents attempting to spell out the economic and social benefits of the disciplines they represent. In their thoroughness, their use of illustrative statistics, and their general air of hard-headed realism, these documents perform their task well enough. But for most of those actually engaged in teaching and scholarship in the humanities, these publications are bound to seem simultaneously a political necessity and a category mistake. Of course, it is understood that these are attempts to use 'the only language which Whitehall will listen to' – that is, the language of contribution to economic prosperity. But as the figures pile up of the amount overseas students pay in fees or the annual revenue of the UK publishing industry or the takings from theatres in Britain, and much more in the same vein, the real value of what they are attempting to justify – what it is that makes these disciplines so interesting that people want to devote their lives to them – seems not just to have been lost sight of but to have been denied any standing, as though it would be naive or embarrassing to talk in such terms. This means that in the end these accounts fail to characterize what is distinctive about the activities they purport to justify. No doubt if one were to tot up the takings generated by Shakespeare, from theatre productions to tea towels, they could be shown to approximate the GDP of a smallish country. Yet no one considers that the *literary* interest and value of his writings would be reduced by one iota if the sum involved was halved or indeed turned out to be to zero. (The worldwide cultural success of 'Shakespeare' over the centuries is an interesting topic in its own right, but that's a different matter.) Similarly, the quality of a good critical study of Shakespeare, or of any other writer, is not determined by, and cannot be assessed in terms of, whether a TV producer happened to be provoked by it into making a programme seen by millions, though the existence of such programmes might be desirable in itself. There is a great danger for the humanities if they put all their eggs in this particular economic basket, since much of the most valuable scholarship in these fields has little or no discernible direct economic outcome. Hence the importance of trying to characterize these disciplines more adequately so that statements of their 'point', if one is driven to that rather desperate task, can be attempted without having to start from premises which are almost bound to neglect or traduce what is of value in them.

We should not, however, allow this observation about the differences in the public purchase of arguments about the sciences and the humanities to lead us to endorse or reinstate any version of the 'two cultures' dichotomy. It is not simply that there is no coherent intellectual basis for this conventional distinction – not in method or subject-matter or purpose – but also, more importantly here, that scholars and scientists share more, and have a greater interest in common where the role of universities is concerned, than the hackneyed contrast tends to suggest. Indeed, as a rough rule of thumb one may say that the more distinguished the scientists are at their science, the more readily they acknowledge the shared character of intellectual enquiry and the more they are willing to make common cause with their colleagues in the humanities against various ways of talking (or measuring) that misrepresent this. 'Two cultures' talk has its main current home, as it had its origins, among those who feel some kind of cultural insecurity about their identities as scientists or among those who administer science rather than doing it (the two groups are not mutually exclusive). Needless to say, for certain everyday practical or institutional purposes it makes sense to follow the traditional rough grouping of disciplines, though this produces awkward definitional problems on both 'sides'. The more applied parts of engineering and medicine are for some purposes lumped in with the physical and biological sciences and for other purposes treated separately (they each have their own national academy, for example), while a phrase such as 'the arts, humanities, and social sciences' attempts to provide an umbrella under which gather rather disparate kinds of subjects that would not be thought to have much in common were it not raining. In London, the British Academy and the Royal Society are next-door neighbours in the same handsome Regency terrace, with some sharing of their facilities – a neatly symbolic expression both of the traditional version of the divide and of their joint standing and joint interests. There are many ways of grouping and subdividing academic disciplines: they do not logically or naturally fall into two mutually exclusive categories. And by the same token all forms of disciplined intellectual enquiry share a common interest where their social value is in question and should make common cause in speaking up for that value.

III

One of the recurring difficulties with nearly all writing about universities, this book included, is the apparent discrepancy or lack of proportion between, on the one hand, the elevated, high-toned rhetoric of the general characterization of their purposes, and, on the other, the necessarily limited and pragmatic accommodation to contemporary circumstances that makes up daily experience in any actual university. This involves more than the familiar, perhaps universal, slippage between ideal and reality. As I suggested earlier, there is something about the uncontainable life of the mind which naturally provokes a kind of verbal excess, a straining beyond the limits of measured or concrete description. But this soaring vocabulary has somehow to be tethered to one set of historically determined institutional arrangements rather than another, and it can then become hard to see how *that* necessarily partial, flawed, and instrumental set of doings can ever yield outcomes that merit such elevated language. In addition, scholarship and teaching have to be about something in particular – about polymers or Dante or social-survey design or quarks or speech-acts or the Bolivian economy or a thousand and one other particular topics – and initially it is not obvious how such radically diverse activities could all be subject to the same canons of intellectual enquiry or issue in anything like comparable educational outcomes.

This general difficulty is only intensified by reflection on the everyday experience of teaching or studying in most British universities in the early twenty-first century. Even if it were granted that in principle some continuity could be found between the bafflingly diverse range of activities now carried on in these institutions and the large claims made for their purpose and value, it might still seem that only the arts of satire or parody could do justice to the conditions under which these activities are often pursued in practice. As I suggested earlier, the sheer scale of the transformation of British higher education in the past twenty years has created a new institutional world, beyond even the altered political and cultural attitudes of which this expansion is the partial expression. Different observers of this new world will, each with some plausibility, select different features of it for praise or criticism. Universities may be seen as more relevant, more inclusive, and more accountable than their predecessors of a generation or two ago; they may equally be seen as less distinctive, less attractive, and less rewarding. They are undeniably more diverse in both types of institution and fields of study, and they are arguably more varied in quality and viability. The declarations of purpose which might, in 1850, have seemed adequate to the existence of Oxford and Cambridge and a handful of Scottish and London colleges, or which might, in 1950, have embraced the broadly homogeneous twenty-three British universities of that time, may seem to be put under more strain by the diversity embraced in the (roughly) 130 universities of today.

However, this apparent diversity actually masks a good deal of continuity in fundamentals. Many new disciplines or sub-disciplines are essentially recombinations of earlier approaches or extensions of existing methods to new subject-matter. A generation or so ago there may have been no university departments labelled 'Neuroscience', but what now goes on under that rubric would have been recognizable to many physiologists, experimental psychologists, brain surgeons and others who passed their working lives within differently named units. Similarly, Cultural Studies may seem to be a novel enterprise which disrupts some of the received understanding of the classification of the humanities and social sciences, but actually it has evolved by re-shaping aspects of its inheritance from sociology, literary criticism, anthropology, and so on, and by applying the resulting approaches to materials that are not different in kind from those studied by, say, social historians or musicologists. And although with all social phenomena there can come a point where, as Marx pointed out long ago, quantitative change becomes qualitative change, brute expansion of numbers alone need not entail any significant alteration of rationale. When we say confidently, as I have done myself, that arrangements that may have worked well when 6% of the age-cohort went to university are bound to work less well when 45% do so, we are usually thinking of such matters as funding or political justification; the character of the disciplined but open-ended enquiry in which the larger numbers now engage may, in principle, have altered very little.

The question of numbers also comes up in other, less predictable ways when arguing about the identity and role of universities. For example, if studying and writing about some aspect of the human or natural world is so interesting and valuable, why don't we get everyone to do it? The obvious impracticability of this at present does not detract from its heuristic value as an uncomfortable question for those who want to make the case for universities. If the things we are standing up for are as valuable and important as we say, why wouldn't we want everyone to study them? Perhaps in some circumstances we would – I see no grounds for specifying a proportion of the population in advance, and certainly no justification for aiming at the 50% participation in higher education specified as the desirable goal by the Blair governments. The Robbins report of 1963 urged that higher education should be available to anyone with the 'potential' to be able to take advantage of it, on the assumption that the number would be higher than the tiny percentage of the age-cohort who currently went to university but perhaps not dramatically higher, and certainly not limitlessly so. In practice, Britain tends to entrust the task of determining who should benefit from higher education at any given time to a combination of A-level exam boards and university admissions tutors; from time to time, when demand from qualified candidates outstrips the number of places universities can offer, a political decision is taken to increase the latter. There is no magic formula to fall back on. The number of university students is arrived at neither by pure demand nor by pure ministerial diktat, but by some mixture of accident, tradition, opportunity, aptitude, resources, and so on. The number may well increase significantly in the next generation or so, but we can never say in advance when the ceiling (of those with the relevant potential) will have been reached. For these reasons among others, our account of what universities are 'for', though it needs to be alert to the changes which growth on this scale brings in its train, should still be applicable whatever the proportion of the population involved. An adequate conception of the university has nothing to fear from expansion; quite the contrary.

At the same time, there can be difficulties of another kind lurking beneath arguments about numbers. For example, even if the case can be made that a particular scholarly or scientific activity is important in itself and an essential part of a wider educational and research pro-gramme, are there any means of deciding how many people should be doing it? This can be rather like asking, say, how many top-class oboists a society should have. How do we decide how many deeply learned scholars in Assyrian archaeology there should be? It is simply silly, or else wilfully obstructive, to reply 'However many the market will bear'. There is no genuine market in such matters: the so-called 'market' is in practice a rigged framework (benevolently rigged, for the most part) which is periodically adjusted if there is expression of one or another form of discontent with existing provision. There is a necessary element of investment in the cultural future involved, and perhaps an educational task in bringing some sections of the popula-tion to recognize this necessity, which market forces simply can never perform. But there can be no general formula for specifying how many of these various specialized people a society should have, beyond perhaps an essential minimum for the survival and transmis-sion of the craft itself. Britain may now have considerably fewer scholars of ancient Greek literature (or at least people with good enough Greek to undertake such scholarship in the original) than it did in 1900 or even 1950. This reduction is explicable and may be entirely appropriate; it has anyway come about as a result of quite large social changes rather than simply by educational fiat. But the question is what *kinds* of consideration should come into play when trying to decide how few is too few, whether in this field or others.

Thus, there is practically no undergraduate 'demand' for the study of, say, ancient Iranian language and literature (and actually a limited range of texts to study in the first place). But there is a formidable scholarly tradition here which surely must not be lost, and which has a wider significance than can be measured by merely citing current undergraduate numbers. Not only do the next generation of scholars of the subject need to be taught, but their expertise needs to be available to those museums and galleries that hold rich collections of Ancient Iranian artworks and artefacts. Scholars in other, perhaps somewhat more popular, areas of ancient Near and Middle Eastern studies depend upon being able to draw on the continuing work of such scholars, as do those working in fields as diverse as comparative linguistics, archaeology, and literary history. Then there is the need for those who comment upon or work in modern Iran to be informed about the presence and influence of such ancient texts in modern cultural attitudes and practices, and so on – the chain of intellectual and cultural implication is long, perhaps endless, and yet it yields us no way of fixing a definite number. At some point, a scholarly institution or a central funding body needs to take a decision based on intellectual rather than merely quantitative considerations. Such decisions depend upon well-argued cases: defensiveness about the very possibility of such arguments can be a fatal starting-point.

IV

Defensiveness of another kind comes into play when universities are asked to demonstrate that they are actually doing what they say they are doing. The peculiarity of the current forms of this demand should not escape comment. Very roughly speaking, universities assist students to educate themselves through the provision of teaching and other scholarly resources, and then determine by various types of examination how well the students have learned. At the same time, the scholars and scientists responsible for the teaching are also advancing the understanding of their disciplines through scholarship and research, and the state of the new understanding arrived at is exhibited in publications and other forms of address to relevant publics. An annual report that all this has indeed happened, together with a statistical and financial summary, may seem to be the only evidence that could be needed – indeed, it may seem to be the only kind of evidence there could be. But the requirement that all this should be verified in some other way expresses once more the suspicious nature of our beady-eyed friend, the taxpayer – or, at least, the use of that bogey-figure for political purposes.

In modern consumerist societies there is a widespread suspicion that any form of self-regulation is bound to be a cloak for complacency and even corruption. The interest of 'the public', it is argued, needs to be enforced by installing mechanisms for properly public scrutiny. And these will tend to be the most mechanical of mechanisms because they must translate complex and elusive human achievements into some kind of measurable 'data' that are comprehensible to a non-expert public. But what if the activity being scrutinized is not, beyond a certain minimal level, susceptible to effective regulation of this kind, since its quality is a matter of informed judgement? In such cases, a substitute has to be found, something that can stand proxy for the real activity so that the appearance of public scrutiny can be maintained. As part of this broader logic, universities in Britain have had to over-invest in the apparently 'objective' and 'transparent' mechanisms of process and assessment in order to demonstrate, to an implicitly sceptical audience, that they are in fact doing what they say they are doing. To satisfy this requirement, universities have, in effect, to misrepresent their own fundamental activities. Consider, for example, the now familiar phrases about how universities must 'assure' the 'delivery' of the syllabus, and so on. There is no need to dwell on the more obvious discrepancies between an education and a pizza to recognize here the dangers of encouraging the users of such language to treat a syllabus, and students' engagement with it, as something inert, something that is simply handed over on the doorstep of their minds. The less obvious point is signalled by the reliance in such bureaucratic rhetoric on the notion of 'assuring' that this delivery has taken place. The risky, unpredictable interaction between minds that has to go on if any genuine education is to happen cannot be, in this sense, 'assured'. The teacher may write a report of what was done in the course, but even that would be bound to stay at one remove from the important reality of the experience. But actually, such a report is not what is required by the current regimes of 'assurance', and recording the experience is not their motivating force. What is asked for now is not any insight into how learning happens or how minds may be enlarged, but a confirmation to third parties that the announced procedures have been followed. It is another example of the fallacy of accountability – that is, the belief that the process of reporting on an activity in the approved form provides some guarantee that something worthwhile has been properly done.

The anxiety that drives such empty formalism is not just yet another expression of the more widespread erosion of trust, though it is also that (the experienced teacher is not trusted to be the best judge of whether and in what ways the students' understandings have been altered by a particular educational experience). It is, in addition, a symptom of the loss of confidence in the possibility of rational argument about the worthwhileness of various human activities. As a result, the pseudo-objectivity of process is substituted for the always contestable exercise of judgement. We persuade ourselves that, for all its imperfections, a regime of 'quality assurance' at least provides some check upon idleness, incompetence, and corruption; we persuade ourselves that 'the public' would not tolerate a situation in which there was not some such form of 'accountability'; we persuade ourselves that this is the least bad outcome. But we are, collectively, mistaken about all this. The great unspoken truth is that the processes of 'assurance' do not actually achieve these ends: they merely indicate that the processes of assurance have been complied with. No matter how carefully a statement about the 'aims and objectives' of a course is drawn up and scrutinized, and no matter how punctiliously the designated officer or committee reports that these aims and objectives were 'delivered', these records tell us nothing of value about what actually happened and provide no reassurance that education was taking place.

The loss of confidence in the possibility of rational argument about the worthwhileness of various human activities ramifies very widely through higher education, though not of course through higher education alone. The reliance on publicly scrutinizable procedures as a substitute for reasoned argument involves an endless deferral of judgement, or at the very least its burial under layers of ostensibly value-neutral bureaucratese. But it should be obvious that, at some point, decisions will still have to be made in terms that are independent of the 'aims and objectives' rhetoric. After all, within the terms of that rhetoric, a perfectly coherent case could be made out for a course in, say, astrology. It would be eminently deliverable, quite possibly very popular, and almost guaranteed to issue in positive student evaluations ('you will find that you enjoy your course despite your initial scepticism'). It might even score quite highly in terms of 'preparation for employment' (careers in banking and the stock market, for example, as well as more directly vocational outcomes in fairgrounds and teen magazines). Unless the faculty or department meeting at which the initial proposal was discussed felt able to appeal to some shared criteria of intellectual validity and significance, there would be no reason in terms of quality-assurance processes to fault the institution and subsequent 'delivery' of such a course.

A further discursive distortion which encumbers current discussion of universities, and which expresses another aspect of this defensiveness, is what has been called the 'no standing still' conception of 'excellence'. Whatever the activity is, it must, we are constantly told, improve at a certain rate. Standards must always be 'driven up'. Benchmarks exist to be surpassed. It becomes difficult, as these phrases insinuate themselves into our thinking, to insist that if something is already being done very well, then the right thing may be to go on doing it like that. Other critics have pointed out the vacuity of 'excellence' as it is used in these contexts: there is no such thing as 'excellence' in the abstract, and it only makes sense as a descriptive term when there is a) agreement about the character and worth of the relevant activity in the first place, and b) some agreed means of arriving at comparative judgements of how far any one instance embodies more of that worth. But vacuity is now rendered more vacuous still by the requirement that the 'excellent' must become 'yet more excellent' on pain of being exposed as complacent or backward-looking or something equally scandalous. (A recent advertisement for a senior administrative post in a British university announced that the appointee would be expected to take the institution 'beyond excellence', which may represent the logical comeuppance of this way of talking.) Although it should go without saying that all human activities constantly adjust themselves to changing circumstances, it now has to be said very emphatically that in many areas of life the notion of 'continuous improvement' is conceptually incoherent.

But these contemporary pathologies can be seen as the index of a deeper problem. There is an ambivalence, sometimes bordering on incoherence, in the attitudes towards universities frequently manifested by politicians and others in what is called 'the policy-making community'. On the one hand, universities are lauded as a source of innovation and creative thinking; it is acknowledged, at least rhetorically, that freedom of enquiry is essential to the discovery of new ideas. But, on the other hand, universities are criticized for the 'self-indulgent' cultivation of 'useless' forms of enquiry; they constantly need to be recalled to the task of serving social needs. Hence the constant dialectic in which universities elaborate subjects in more and more 'academic' directions while governments seek to impose other priorities and to devise forms of regulation in a (partly doomed) attempt to enforce these priorities. This is an unresolvable tension, an attempt to govern the ungovernable. In effect, universities are frequently being exhorted: 'Be original – but in the right way.'

Increasingly, only one right way is countenanced: it is coming to be taken not merely as appropriate or desirable in some cases but as *self-evident* that we have to show how any publicly funded activity 'serves the needs of the economy'. However, there is nothing self-evident about this supposed requirement; quite the contrary. As I have already suggested, it begs the question of what needs the economy serves. And if the answer is said to be, no less self-evidently, that the economy provides the means which enables us to do the things we consider really important, then we clearly need to begin by having some sense of what is really important and then tailor our economic activities accordingly. Much contemporary discourse finds itself in the self-defeating position of arguing that the carrying-on of activity A is justified only if it can be shown to contribute to making more money, while acknowledging that the purpose of making more money is to enable us to continue doing things such as carrying on activity A.

Clearly, the fundamental difficulty lies in the unchallenged position of 'prosperity' as a goal, a topic beyond the scope of this book. But if economic activity is principally a means to something else, a way of amassing the resources with which to do things which have more interest and significance for human beings than economic activity itself does, then rather than saying that extending human understanding is valuable because it provides the means to prosperity we should surely say that one of the reasons prosperity is valuable is because it provides the wherewithal to extend human understanding. Otherwise we risk heading further towards that condition satirized long ago by Keynes in which we become 'capable of shutting off the sun and the stars because they do not pay a dividend'.

PART TWO

Prologue: Occasions for Advocacy

Universities need advocates. As we have seen, there is nothing self-evident about their character, their functions, or their value. As more is expected of them, and as more public funds are devoted to sustaining them, they are, inevitably, subjected to increasing levels of scrutiny. In Britain their activities are now the object of unprecedented media coverage as well as of a historically unparalleled degree of political regulation. And this, as those who teach in universities have become all-too-painfully aware in recent years, is where the need for advocates comes in. The sheer volume of ignorance, misunderstanding, and hostility which marks so much public and political comment on universities at present cries out for correction and rebuttal. But it is not obvious who should be responsible for this task, or by what means it is best undertaken. Academics are busier than ever simply carrying the burdens of increased teaching loads, unstoppably multiplying administrative procedures, and the assessment-driven obligation to yet more publication. And in any case, many academics may not be particularly well-suited, either by inclination or training, to engage in the kind of polemical writing or speaking in the national media which may be required. As a result, an additional reproach is now levelled at those in academia: if universities have been damaged by inappropriate or misguided policies, academics have, it is said, no one to blame but themselves. They have let the case for their activities go by default. If they are not willing to speak out, to challenge such policies, and to attempt to enlist public support for more enlightened approaches then, say their accusers, they must live with the consequences of their timidity, indifference, and self-absorption.

The chapters in Part Two of this book constitute an attempt, or series of attempts, at such speaking out. With one exception, they have all been published in earlier forms (most of Chapter 7 has not previously been published but is based on two talks for BBC Radio 3). I am all too aware how limited a contribution such short and opportunistic forays can make. They were initially written as responses to particular episodes in the fraught and unequal relationship between universities and government over the past couple of decades. I bring them together here partly in an effort to get a wider audience to attend to their arguments, but partly as a small demonstration of the untruth of the accusation I have just summarized. And I should emphasize that I have been nothing like a lone voice; in fact I have been a much quieter and more intermittent voice than certain admirable colleagues who have spoken out along broadly similar lines over the years. It is simply not true that all academics have been silent on these matters.

Nonetheless, the effect of these arguments and objections on those who make and implement policies for universities has been, as far as I can judge, all but invisible. A note of rueful realism is bound to enter our reflections at this point. Over the past couple of decades there has been a considerable body of cogent and compelling criticism of the various measures that have so damaged British universities, from the imposition of corporate governance structures to the successive waves of misguided assessment procedures. An outside observer would be bound to conclude that the critics have, as the fashionable phrase has it, 'won the intellectual argument'. Yet if so, this has been a bitterly hollow victory, since the widely remarked public statement of these compelling and often devastating criticisms appears to have had little or no effect on policy-making. The arguments have not been answered; they have merely been ignored. Rather than blaming academics for not speaking out sufficiently strongly, the conclusion which is much more consistent with the evidence is that those who make policy are just not listening.

Of course, we all understand, in general terms, that it takes tireless efforts at lobbying, networking, campaigning, and generally being a nuisance to have any effect on the decisions of politicians and their advisers. No one expects policy to be changed overnight simply as a result of a single article, however well-argued. Everyone understands that the formation and implementation of policy towards higher education is a long-term business, drawing on various levels of debate and consultation, and subject to political, financial, and electoral constraints. But this should also mean that there are many groups involved in these processes who are, or certainly ought to be, more susceptible than a busy minister can always be to various forms of reasoned objection. Such criticism may sometimes take the form of showing that the categories and starting-points involved in some proposal are inappropriate and will end up distorting what they aim to regulate. But no less often there is scope for what philosophers call 'immanent criticism', that is, showing that even if the premises of a proposal are accepted in themselves, they prove to be self-contradictory and will be self-frustrating when applied. Civil servants, policy advisers, officials in higher education quangos, and university administrators are particularly vulnerable to criticism of this sort because they have both to explain and justify policy at the outset and then to make sure that it works. No intelligent administrators want to be saddled with a proposal which they know to be visibly flawed, open to cogent objection, and not likely to obtain the support of those to whom it is to be applied. Critics of higher education polices in Britain do not, therefore, need to entertain the implausibly insiderish fantasy that they must 'have the ear' of Peter Mandelson or David Willetts or whoever happens to be temporarily charged with political responsibility for such policies. It is more realistic, and in the long run may be more effective, to focus on that intermediate level of public discussion where those who have to carry out policies are forced to confront the evidence of incoherence and unjustifiability.

Even at this level, however, the need for good arguments to be repeated, and then repeated again, can be dispiriting. One of the lessons to be drawn from reflecting on, for example, the sad history of misguided forms of assessment of research in universities, from the fad for 'bibliometry' in the late 1980s to the fad for 'impact' in the late 2000s, is that the same kinds of category mistake are made over and over again, which therefore need to be countered by re-stating the same first principles involved in understanding the activity of 'research', and indeed of 'assessment'. In the world of science and scholarship, repeating the same argument, re-using the same material, even re-publishing previously published work, all tend to be frowned upon as redundant or self-indulgent. A scholarly case once properly made and substantiated can then be consulted by anyone interested in the topic: there is no need to re-state it since the original remains both authoritative and accessible. But the world of public polemic is not like that. John Stuart Mill long ago observed that 'an article in a newspaper is to the public mind no more than a drop of water on a stone; and like that it produces its effect by *repetition*.' The clichés and canards that plague the discussion of universities in Britain are pervasive and long-lived; they need to be repeatedly confronted with truer accounts, even with the same true account in some cases. I hope, therefore, that it is a strength rather than a weakness of the pieces included here that they sometimes repeat fundamentally similar points in only slightly different terms. Those involved in foisting damaging measures on universities are not themselves fastidious about repetition. The very strong case which universities have for the distinctiveness and value of what they do should not be allowed to go by default just because there seems no need, it having once been well stated in the past, to rehearse it again. The time to stop repeating it will be when it has been properly attended to. That time does not seem very near.

It is true that because there is now so much writing about higher education, and such constant assertions that it is 'in crisis', returning to aspects of the topic in this critical vein risks the fate of the boy who cried wolf. As W. B. Carnochan observed some years ago, speaking of general accounts of the condition of universities in the United States: 'We have reached a situation of diminishing returns in which the apparent sameness of the argument undermines some of its vitality (if not volume), even its interest, while obscuring the possibility of an analysis that would distinguish what is merely repetitious from what is – however analogous to earlier debate – qualitatively different and dependent on new circumstances in the society.' I can only hope that these chapters, while undeniably exhibiting 'apparent sameness of argument', also draw attention to what is qualitatively different in each case.

One further reason for re-publishing them risks, I admit, seeming either sentimental or self-important, but I am moved by the fact that each of these pieces produced, on their original publication, a quite astonishing volume of letters and comment, far in excess of the response I have received to anything else I have ever done or written – a response not just from academics themselves, but also from journalists, writers, and members of the general public, both in Britain and overseas. This response was overwhelmingly, indeed almost unanimously, supportive, even in some cases going on to elaborate further failings in the policies which I had tried to challenge. But more significant, I have come to think, was the tone of delight and vindication that marked these communications, especially among academics – a sense of relief that someone had expressed publicly convictions which they deeply shared but which they had scarcely dared admit to in their own universities. In this respect, the messages were pleasing but also disturbing. After all, what I have to say in these chapters is, as I emphasize more than once, neither original nor eccentric: these are, or should be, commonplaces, yet here were large numbers of academics in British universities feeling that to utter such truisms out loud might be as incriminating, perhaps even as consequential, as shouting patriotic slogans in the face of an occupying army.

I have therefore decided to leave each of these chapters pretty much in the form in which it was originally written. Obviously, this means that in places my allusions or my use of tenses will appear out of date – in these chapters 'now' does not mean now and the 'present government' is not the present government. The reader must bear in mind the dates of original composition in each case (respectively, 1989, 2000/06, 2003, 2009, and 2010). But although some details of the particular proposals under discussion may now seem irrelevant, the principles animating these policies seem all too hideously familiar, and thus, as I argued in the Introduction, it still seems worth trying to bring more adequate principles to bear by way of criticism. Since all but one of these critiques take issue with official documents, I have given the details of these publications at the start of each chapter, at the foot of the page.

6

Bibliometry

I

Not everything that counts can be counted. It's true that where the catch-phrase of late-nineteenth-century politics was 'We are all socialists now', the motto (epitaph?) of our age seems rather to be 'We are all accountants now'. Yet, perverse as it may seem, there are issues where the most important among the things that cannot be counted are the costs. The question of 'performance indicators' in universities is one such issue. But perhaps, sensing what is to follow, you are already starting to feel impatient: 'Doesn't he realize that this is the way the world is run these days, and we either work within their categories or we pay the cost?' *Their* categories? *The* cost? Now read on.

Under the joint auspices of the Committee of Vice-Chancellors and Principals (CVCP) and the University Grants Committee (UGC),[1] a sub-committee has been set up to carry out a 'pilot scheme' preparatory to developing 'a methodology for counting and classifying

1 The CVCP later became Universities UK (UUK), while the UGC was replaced by, initially, the University Funding Council (UFC), which in turn was quickly replaced by the Higher Education Funding Council for England (HEFCE; the other parts of the UK have matching councils). It should soon be possible to write a coherent sentence about higher education entirely in acronyms.

University Management Statistics and Performance Indicators in the UK (London: the Committee of Vice-Chancellors and Principals, 1988)

publications'. The membership of this sub-committee is published in the 1988 edition of *University Management Statistics and Performance Indicators in the UK*. It comprises two Vice-Chancellors and one Registrar, two specialists in science policy, a professor each of Physics, Chemistry, and Financial Management (good to see the Arts have not been forgotten), and eight administrators from the Department of Education and Science, UGC, and other such bodies. In the 'Introduction' to its 'Pilot Survey of Research Publications', the sub-committee tells us that 'those consulted so far accept that one thing is crucial – the need to establish a database of research output ... on which appropriate bibliometric methods can be demonstrated'. Perhaps, in that case, a little more 'consulting' might not come amiss.

The four subjects selected for the pilot survey are physics, chemistry, economics, and history. Forms and notes on their completion have been sent out, asking for a full list of staff, a full list of publications, and a 'statistical summary' (glossed as: 'A numerical summary of the full bibliography on the form provided. For each specified subject a single row of figures should appear in each half of the table'). The object, we are told, is 'to seek suggestions on matters of principle and practice to ensure that the eventual format is as satisfactory as possible'. The eventual use to which the 'appropriate bibliometric methods' will be put is not explained. The accompanying letter speaks of 'promot[ing] studies of ways in which bibliometric methods can be used to assist judgements of research'. Just 'assist', you understand; nothing drastic.

Perhaps a little more light is cast – well, all right, not exactly 'light' – by the minute of the CVCP meeting noting the proposal to conduct the pilot scheme. 'The ultimate objective', it explains is 'for there to be quantitative data on publications in every university department, but this would only be an adjunct to the traditional quantitative forms of peer group assessment of research.' I'm sorry, I'll read that again. No, it doesn't matter which way up you hold it, it still seems to be saying that we used to do it by counting publications, but now we've had this super new wheeze and we're going to do it by ... counting publications (counting better? more systematically? differently?). Not quite what I had imagined 'traditional peer group assessment of research' to be like. Ah, but perhaps all is explained by the hypothesis that 'traditional quantitative forms' in the latter part of that sentence is a slip of the CVCP pen for 'traditional qualitative forms'? Slips of the pen, are of course, like slips of the tongue, simply accidental and reveal nothing; certainly nothing to worry about in the fact that the administrators of the CVCP write 'quantitative' when they mean 'quantitative'.

'All right, smart-arse, you've had your fun; but what's the alternative? We know that the Cabinet Office has demanded that we come up with measures of "productivity" in universities [sorry about the quotation-marks, I know it's like throwing a handful of flowers at an advancing tank]. How else are we going to measure it?'

Well, let's start there. We don't *measure* it; we *judge* it. Understanding that distinction, really understanding it, is the first step of wisdom in these matters. And what is 'it'? 'Research Productivity'? Just think about that phrase for a moment – and then we can agree to start somewhere else.

The impulse behind the UGC/CVCP pilot scheme is financial and managerial. The amount of time spent on 'research', so we are told, has to be distinguished from the amount of time spent on 'teaching' (these are apparently the only two activities conducted in universities), so that 'resources' can be assigned to each. 'Research selectivity' involves finding out which 'cost centres' are good at 'research', or at least do a lot of it, or at least publish a lot of it, so that the amount of money which other institutions receive for the 'research' they're not very good at, or at least not doing enough of, or at least not publishing enough of, can be reduced. An exercise like this innocuous-seeming pilot scheme is, therefore, highly consequential. More generally, what is fundamentally at issue is the adequacy of the categories in terms of which we are being asked to represent our activities to ourselves and others. How appropriate are the categories proposed in this pilot scheme, and what do they suggest about the assumptions and purposes of those who have framed them?

I'm afraid we have once again to start with the very category of 'research' itself – 'afraid' because many may think it obstructive or quixotic even to express any reservations about this fundamental category. But while we are no doubt committed to using the word, we have to be careful not to let it bring in its train assumptions and expectations which are damagingly inappropriate. It has to be said – and has to be said now more emphatically than ever – that in many areas of the humanities 'research' can be a misleading term. It is difficult to state briefly how work in these areas should be characterized, but we are at least pointed in the right direction by phrases such as 'cultivating understanding', 'nurturing and extending a cultural heritage', 'thinking critically about the profoundest questions of human life', and so on. Both publication and teaching are in a sense dependent on this more fundamental activity, however we characterize it, and are natural and inseparable expressions of it; but the activity itself is not reducible without remainder to those two categories. Publication in the humanities is, therefore, not always a matter of communicating 'new findings' or proposing a 'new theory'. It is often the expression of the deepened understanding which some individual has acquired, through much reading, discussion, and reflection, on a topic which has been in some sense 'known' for many generations.

Things are, I am quite willing to believe, different in the sciences, and even to some extent in the social sciences. (For this reason it is unfortunate that the two 'arts' subjects chosen for this exercise should be economics and history; the limits of its appropriateness might be even more sharply defined if it were addressed to, say, philosophy or one of the literature-based disciplines.) Even so, it is revealing of the difficulties any uniform scheme will encounter that one very senior scientist whom I spoke to about it immediately replied: 'Well, the main problem is that the categories are obviously designed to reflect research in the arts', remarking, for example, the way the category of 'review' or 'review-article' really has no standing in his field, where it suggests, if it suggests anything, an appraisal of a research-team or grant application. The head of another large scientific research-group complained that: 'The authors of the questionnaire have not thought it out properly in advance', urging that it was misleading in certain areas of team and collaborative research to try to list publications by individuals. What all this suggests, surely, is that we need to be alert to the differences *among* the various activities carried on in universities, and to ensure that we judge excellence in their conduct accordingly. This pilot scheme does just the opposite.

The premise of the exercise is that the categories must be uniform. For the purposes of developing 'bibliometric methods' it is no good whingeing that editing early-medieval Latin texts is a touch different from conducting research in particle physics; just make sure we have a number in each box, will you? Even leaving aside for the moment the question of the point of such an exercise and the uses to which the 'data' will be put, and even leaving aside the whole question of judgements of quality and significance to be made between publications, it should still be obvious that even for the task of simply *recording* the publications of those working in universities, a far more variegated and nuanced set of categories would be required. Where are we to place activities, crucial to others' scholarship, such as compiling dictionaries or editing texts? In which box do we report the creative role of the editor of a collaborative volume or the critical role of the editor of a literary journal? How do we record that seminal review-essay in the *New York Review of Books* or that letter to the *Times Literary Supplement* definitively demolishing a purported new edition of some classic text? What sense does it make in the humanities to propose classifying journals as either 'academic', 'professional', or 'popular'? What does it mean to limit entries under 'other media' to 'work which represents a contribution to research'? Is it irrelevant that our literary critics write poems and novels, that our historians develop TV documentaries, that our economists challenge official statistics in the weeklies, and so on? Many more objections of this kind might be made, and I can only hope that some of the departments involved in this pilot scheme have had sufficient self-respect to make them.

But again the Voice of Realism pipes up: 'Surely it is not unreasonable to ask those employed at public expense to provide some record of their activities? Or is it only those with something to hide who object to proper records being kept?' For the moment we may ignore the innuendoes and question-begging aspects of this all-too-familiar refrain, but it does invite us to probe a little more deeply the purpose of this exercise.

No one would suggest that we should not collectively keep records of our publications. That we do already. The question is, what difference will the development of 'bibliometric methods' make? If the answer is: 'Don't worry, it won't make any difference at all – it just means keeping records of our publications,' then there would be no need for pilot schemes and the rest of it. Plainly, it is intended to enable us (let's keep the polite fiction of 'us' for the moment) to do something we don't already do. Like what? Judge which departments are doing good research? I don't believe that anyone has ever suggested that those conducting peer-review exercises should be *denied* material which would be helpful to arriving at an informed judgement. Ah, but now the 'data' will be more precise; for example, an assessing committee will be able to tell at a glance how many publications *in each category* various comparable departments have. Oh yes, we agree that the categories are never going to be perfect, but only if we have a uniform system of classification can comparative assessments of departments be made.

But wait a minute, the point about *peer* review is that they are just the people who understand about publications in the field in question: they are the people who know what weight to attach to various kinds of publications in that discipline, they are the ones who know which are the good journals, and so on. 'Bibliometric methods' will not provide any 'objective' criteria here; they will simply iron out differences in category appropriate to each discipline. There is, in other words, no point in trying to devise a set of categories of publication appropriate to all disciplines unless you intend to reduce the extent to which decisions rest on judgement by peers and increase the extent to which they rest on measurement by administrators. It is not just that someone still has to discriminate a good piece of work from a mediocre one, or that there might be other considerations altogether to take into account in making the decision. It is that a uniform set of categories will be an obstacle and not an adjunct to making peer-group assessments. Those qualified to make such an assessment will have in effect to ignore the categories the 'database' presents and recognize what a review-essay or a letter to *Nature* or whatever means in their own field.

So, the clear implication is that this information will be used to make decisions, primarily about funding, by those who are not qualified to judge (if they are qualified to judge, then casting the information into inappropriate uniform categories will only be a hindrance). 'Bibliometric methods' will provide a spurious sense of judging by objective criteria. This is borne out by the 'research selectivity' exercise now under way. The UGC lists four criteria by which the 'ratings' of the various 'cost centres' will be determined. The second and third of these are the predictable 'market-forces' indicators: success in obtaining research grants and students, and success in obtaining research contracts (a great way to sort out departments of, say, philosophy or classics). The fourth criterion – not the first, note – is 'professional knowledge and judgement of advisory group and panel members, supplemented where appropriate by advice from outside experts'. This, I take it, is what most of us understand, roughly speaking, by 'peer review'. So what is the first criterion? 'Publication and other publicly identifiable output'. The fact that this is given as a quite separate criterion from that of 'professional knowledge and judgement' gives the whole game away.

II

Further down the line, of course, stands the spectre of the 'Citation Index', which is what most people understand by 'bibliometric methods' (if they understand anything by it at all). The CVCP have not made clear whether they regard the present 'initiative' (a word fallen on hard times if ever there was one) as an alternative to counting citation-frequency or as a step towards it. The latter seems the more plausible answer, alas, so for those of you who have led sheltered lives up till now it may be worth explaining that it involves, roughly (oh, so roughly) speaking, establishing the significance of a piece of work by totting up how often it appears in the footnotes in other people's journal articles. I agree, I didn't believe it when I first heard about it. Apparently, there are one or two areas in the sciences where this produces a fairly reasonable guide to the importance of the 'new findings' in a given publication. The idiocy involved in using this as an indicator of anything of importance in most fields is too obvious to need rehearsing.

However, since in these dark days we need things to cheer us up, let me just report that the whole business can be sabotaged with ridiculous ease. All you do, of course, is simply to fill your publications with more references to the work of your friends or of other members of your department or of other members of your citation cooperative or of people you know are in danger of losing their jobs because a crack-brained scheme has determined they should unless their citation-rate goes up. In the United States there are now said to be 'citation-rings' in those fields where any weight is placed upon this pottiness. One can even imagine the kinds of advertisements one would find in the samizdat publications giving the names of those in need of citations: 'You could prevent a child going hungry this Christmas. Just one reference to a publication by its parent . . .'

Yet even if we are not led down the cul-de-sac of citation-counting, the introduction of 'bibliometric methods' will, in indirect and perhaps less obvious ways, have more generally damaging consequences on the quality of the intellectual activity carried on in British universities. There can be no doubt that if 'bibliometric methods' are pursued (and it is still not too late for the UGC/CVCP to acknowledge that the whole idea is misconceived), then this will very significantly increase pressure on those in universities to increase the *quantity* of their publications. This will be demonstrably harmful to the 'excellence' which, in other of its pronouncements, the UGC declares itself to be committed to fostering. Again, one would have thought this was too obvious to need spelling out. Scholarly activity in the humanities requires time; making everyone so jittery that they suffer from *publicatio praecox* will no more improve the quality of our intellectual life than a faster 'rate of production' of ejaculations would necessarily improve our sexual lives. It will, for example, make it more difficult, especially for younger scholars, to think of undertaking a major project which might not yield any entries for the annual return for several years to come, but which might when completed be worth far more than a whole CVful of slight articles and premature 'syntheses'. Moreover, the ethos encouraged by the overvaluing of quantity in publication will have a pernicious effect upon the other judgements which we are continually called upon to make in academic life. This ethos would, for instance, put considerable pressure on a head of department to appoint to a new post that candidate who is most likely to increase the volume of the department's publications in the shortest time, and so on.

Since it is said, both by those who would welcome as well as those who would regret such an outcome, that developments of this kind will make academic life in Britain more closely resemble that in the United States, it may be as well to address directly the preconceptions and prejudices called up by this prediction. I have no wish to encourage that kind of condescending snobbishness still sometimes found in British universities (and not just in universities) towards what is dismissed as American 'vulgarity' and 'earnestness'. In many fields the fact is that far more of the really significant work is done in the US than in Britain; the current 'brain-drain' is testimony to this, among other things. But an even larger proportion of the bad work is done there too, and there is no doubt that a greater emphasis in various forms of career assessment upon quantity of publication encourages this. We are all familiar with the inflexibility with which some American college Deans (administrators, incidentally, and not genuinely 'peers') apply quantitative measures of publication; when 'no book' means 'no tenure', you get a book published whether it's ready or not. Inevitably, this leads to a great many unnecessary and inadequate publications. This does nobody any good; it does the people who write it some harm; it wastes the time of other scholars and students; it costs libraries and other institutions a lot of money.

The motor for the whole misconceived business is the market-ethos of US academic life, where quantity of publication (what the UGC so delicately terms 'publicly identifiable output') has come to be allowed excessively to determine 'market value'. It is revealing that it is only the very best American universities which are prepared to be flexible and to back informed judgement against bibliography-measuring ('this young philosopher has only published two articles, but he/she is so good we are going to give him/her tenure anyway'), and that is because they are the only ones which can afford the self-confidence needed to do so. In pursuing 'bibliometric methods' we shall not be adopting the practices of the most admirable and distinguished universities in the United States, but rather we shall be inadvertently importing some of those aspects of American academic life which are least worth emulating.

III

When a body notionally responsible for promoting and fostering the purposes for which universities exist engages in a course of action manifestly likely to misrepresent and ultimately harm those activities, we are bound to wonder why. Three possible explanations suggest themselves.

The first is that they genuinely do not understand the nature of much of what goes on in the institutions for which they are responsible, and so do not realize that they are misrepresenting it. This is certainly possible. Quite what scholarship in the humanities is 'about' is, as I have already acknowledged, notoriously hard to say, and it is very difficult to justify in terms of economic growth or technological development, which now seem to be the only terms offered by some of the hard-faced accountants sitting round the relevant tables. But if this is the case, then obviously we only make things worse by sending in our returns in the categories asked for, since this will simply confirm the administrators in their misunderstanding.

The second possible explanation is that the members of the UGC and the CVCP understand very well that this and related exercises – no one pretends that this scheme can be considered in isolation from other government-prompted 'rationalization exercises' – are likely in the long run to restrict the intellectual independence of universities, to reduce support for scholarship in the humanities, and to damage the ethos of British academic life. (Indeed, the run may seem uncomfortably short if you happen to be, say, a Lecturer in Philosophy at Hull [a department which was threatened with closure at the time].) But it may be their genuine conviction that this is what should be done. They may, for example, believe that the humanities are not 'real subjects', or that public funds should not be spent on activities which bring no demonstrable economic benefits. In which case we must oblige them to make these convictions manifest. We may at least find some small solace in the international chorus of contempt which will then greet this expression of narrow-minded philistinism.

The third, less drastic, explanation is that some members of these two bodies recognize well enough that these and other recent measures are harmful to many of our activities, but feel that it would be imprudent or pointless to say so. Before rushing off to mount our moral high horses, I think we must extend a limited measure of sympathy to this position. Those in positions of such responsibility have an obligation to be realistic, and those of us not in the hot seats should not be in too much of a hurry to distinguish realism from cowardice. Nonetheless, part of the reason why individuals in these exposed positions may be reluctant to speak out is that they fear they would get little support from the majority of colleagues in less exposed positions, where responses seem, on present showing, to reflect some mixture of fear, apathy, and narrow self-interest. If this is the most nearly correct explanation, it is clear what our response should be. If this genuinely *is* a 'pilot' project, then the CVCP has to be told to find the ejector seat before it's too late. We have to start from the recognition that the nature of the activities carried on in universities is not such as to issue in something describable as 'productivity'; we have to go on to point out that that activity can be judged but not measured; and we have to insist that 'bibliometric methods' will be a hindrance rather than a help to those who are properly capable of making such judgements.

It is no secret that the present Government is hostile to universities and is determined to reduce their real autonomy. Reflecting on the achievements of the Government's second term of office, Mr Norman Tebbit, then Chairman of the Conservative Party, was well satisfied with the progress made in taming institutions like the trade unions and local authorities, but the universities, he observed, had been allowed to be foot-draggingly obstructive: the third term would see to that. The language used by Mr Robert Jackson, the ironically titled 'Minister *for* Higher Education', in his recent Chevening discussion paper on '"Manpower Planning" in Higher Education' indicates chillingly enough what's now coming over the loudspeakers. Having observed that it was infuriatingly difficult to get universities to change their 'hallowed academic practices', he went on: 'Instead, if we are to reduce unit costs to the public purse, we must find ways of obliging the higher education suppliers themselves to address the problem more realistically.' Elsewhere, Mr Jackson has spoken of 'the process of national renovation which is now underway', of which these changes in the position of universities, we are to understand, are an essential part. Perhaps one should not see too much significance in these phrases, which are just the sound of busy politicians reaching for the nearest cliché, but one cannot help recalling that the twentieth century's experience of the consequences of the language of 'national renovation' has not been a happy one.

It was said in occupied France during the Second World War that one way to tell *collaborateurs* from *résistants* was that the former used the bureaucratic terminology of the occupying power without grimacing. The language of many of the documents issuing from the UGC these days sends the mind reaching for such historical illumination. At one point, the letter accompanying the UGC/CVCP pilot survey speaks of 'the need to establish a database of research output which has the confidence of the academic community'. The plain fact is that the recent behaviour of the UGC has gone a long way towards forfeiting that confidence. One way in which it might start to regain it would be to return to using categories and concepts which suggest an adequate understanding of the activities which an academic community exists to promote in the first place. Until the UGC shows some sign of recognizing this truth, the charge of *Pétainisme* will remain to be answered.

7
The Business Analogy

I

I work in the knowledge and human-resources industry. My company specializes in two kinds of product: we manufacture high-quality, multi-skilled units of human capacity; and we produce commercially relevant, cutting-edge new knowledge in user-friendly packages of printed material. I hold a middle-management-level position, responsible to a divisional head who reports directly to the Chief Executive. We have been increasing output of both products during the last twenty years, while at the same time pursuing a cost-cutting programme by making efficiency gains of 1% per year. We compete in the global market-place and our brand-recognition scores are high. The company's name is HiEdBiz plc, and its motto is: 'World-class products at rock-bottom prices'.

Let me put that another way. I'm a university teacher. I teach students and I write books. I'm part of what used to be a largely self-governing community of scholars. We still take it in turns to fill the local administrative roles; in principle we all belong to the university's governing body, with the right to speak there, and we elect a number of representatives from among ourselves to sit on the university's executive council. The intensity of the teaching we do and the quality

---

The first three sections of this chapter are based on two talks given on BBC Radio 3 in February and March 2000.

of the things we write have in some respects declined over the last twenty years, since we don't now have the time to do either properly. I teach at a British university. We don't have a motto.

At least, we didn't used to, aside from a Latin phrase or two on crests and the like. We do, however, now have a 'mission statement'. That's not, as you might think, a declaration about the duty to convert the heathen to the true religion. It's – well, it's hard to say what it is: it's a kind of cross between an extended dictionary definition of the term 'university' and an advertising brochure for an upmarket health club. The 'mission statement' appears in the glossy Annual Report which my university now publishes every year. It also now publishes an Alumni Magazine which contains a lot of the same information, but aimed at former students of the university. If visitors from Mars tried to work out what the place was about, just from the numerous eye-catching pictures these publications contain, they would be likely to conclude that there were two main kinds of people there: there are ones with grey hair, mostly men, who spend their time peering into microscopes, and there are younger ones, mostly women, who divide their time between drinking in a bar, listening to one of the silver-haired men talking, and rowing in a weirdly narrow long boat with big oars. The buildings all look like churches or castles, except for those that look like airport hotels. The word most frequently used in the accompanying bits of prose is 'excellence', especially 'international excellence', which is presumably better still, or perhaps just better in more places. And as an insert there's what looks like a membership form. You agree to pay a certain amount of money to the place each year, and in return, as far as I can see, there's a weekend where you, too, get to go and listen to one of the grey-haired men talking and then to have dinner with a lot of other members in one of the castles. There's no mention of the beery, boating girls at this point, which is probably wise.

It's not surprising that there's a lot of confusion about what universities are and what they're for. For one thing, the nature of intellectual activity itself is quite hard to characterize and pin down; and for another, the institutions we call universities carry out a diverse range of activities under such headings as education, research, professional training, and so on. But one of the main sources of confusion these days is the misleading analogy between a university and a commercial company. We have become so used to this analogy that we hardly notice it any more, nor do we much notice how many of the terms used in speaking about higher education are in fact transplants from the commercial world. But in fact we are constantly asked to 'measure our productivity', to demonstrate the 'value added' by our teaching, to clarify the 'line-management structure' of our administration, to quantify our 'public output', to accelerate our 'student throughput', to increase our 'brand recognition', and much more in the same vein. In particular, universities are increasingly required to operate with a narrowly financial or commercial notion of 'efficiency' which is equated with increased output at reduced cost.

Analogies are always potentially treacherous figures of speech. As Coleridge nicely put it: 'Analogies never walk on all fours,' or in other words analogies inevitably illuminate some hitherto unnoticed similarities while at the same time obscuring real differences. Argument by analogy is defined in the *Oxford English Dictionary* as 'a process of reasoning based upon the assumption that if things have some similar attributes, their other attributes will be similar'. So, universities are like companies in that both organizations have an annual budget: therefore, universities must be like companies in that both organizations have a measurable annual output. The premise is true; the conclusion is false.

One of the supposed benefits of treating universities as though they were businesses is that their efficiency can then be measured and improved. It's well known that universities used to be full of idle, port-swilling dons and equally idle, unemployable students, but now they are lean and mean and geared to meeting national needs through increased productivity. One thing that needs saying in the face of this self-deluded and self-important twaddle is that in several important ways universities are now *less* efficient than they were twenty years ago before the commercial analogy started to be applied in earnest. After all, two of the most important sources of efficiency in intellectual activity are voluntary cooperation and individual autonomy. But these are precisely the kinds of things for which a bureaucratic system leaves little room. We all certainly *report* on ourselves much more fully than we did twenty or thirty years ago, but the unintended by-product of that may be that we concentrate our energies a bit more on doing things that are reportable. It is a mistake to think that if you make people more accountable for what they do, you will necessarily be making them more efficient at doing it.

The talk of 'accountability' and 'productivity' brings with it further assumptions about how to make the place work more 'efficiently'. One is an emphasis on surveillance to make sure nobody is loafing; the other is a system of 'incentive payments' to make people compete with each other. No doubt most organizations contain a few people who don't really pull their weight, but I have to say that in my experience of universities loafing is not exactly the main problem. The kinds of people who go on to do academic research tend to be natural obsessives, prone to waking up too early in the morning worrying about the paragraph they wrote yesterday, or neglecting their partners and families by going in to their labs and offices at the weekend to monitor their experiments or check their footnotes. A system of surveillance designed to make sure that people didn't *over-work* might actually contribute something towards so-called 'efficiency'. Similarly, the idea that encouraging competition among colleagues for some anyway pretty minimal financial rewards is the best way to stimulate intellectual activity reveals a lack of understanding of what creative work is like. Cooperation and a sense of shared commitment to the enterprise is infinitely more fruitful, and anyone who has mixed much with academics will know that, at the individual level, intellectual vanity is a much stronger motivating force than money.

Some of what I am saying here is specific to universities, but some of it raises questions about models of human motivation more generally. If you are a slave-owner, driving a slave-gang, then deterrence of slacking is your chief concern. Efficiency means making them work as hard as possible. Your chattels have no incentive to labour except avoidance of the lash. It's true that you can also try offering the incentive of giving a larger share of the fixed amount of food to those who work hardest, at the expense of nourishing the others, but you'll probably find that they then start fighting among themselves and that some of your workforce die prematurely. So, constant surveillance backed up by the whip is the way to keep them at it. On the other hand, if you are a group of friends, writing, producing, and performing a play in your local village hall, quite the opposite principle applies. You need to do everything you can to stimulate each other's creativity, cooperativeness, and sense of commitment. Rewards for some at the expense of others will be counterproductive, and it's hardly going to help matters if the local council sends someone round each evening to measure your vocal production and your role-playing skills.

Obviously, universities don't correspond to either of these models – there's the danger of analogies again – but their working principles are in some ways nearer to the second example than to the first. The free play of the mind, which is at the heart of academic activity, is not best encouraged by threats. You're more likely to get someone to do fruitful work if you say to them: 'This is an interesting and difficult problem of the kind you're good at, so take your time and let me know if I can be of any help,' than if you say: 'Be creative or I'll beat the hell out of you.'

Part of the problem is that we live in a public culture obsessed with the idea that we must at all costs prevent scroungers and layabouts existing at, as it's always put, 'the taxpayer's expense'. 'Efficiency', on this view, consists in catching them out and making sure that anyone who receives any payment is in exchange doing the work they're contracted to do. That always sounds reasonable enough in itself, but the danger is that this sets up a false antithesis. We soon get into the position of saying that *either* we have a proper system of public accountability by which we measure productivity *or* we have a whingeing, self-indulgent interest-group squandering public money. What, among other things, we need is a more intelligent conception of 'efficiency' than this mechanical 'value-for-money' model. We need to understand how 'efficiency' can mean the set of arrangements that best stimulates and coordinates human energies, and this will vary from activity to activity, from organization to organization.

But, more than this, we also need a public language in which to describe and justify the value of what we do. The other day I was reading a publication by the Arts and Humanities Research Board [later to become a full research council, the AHRC], the body set up to fund advanced research in the humanities roughly along the lines of the councils which fund research in the natural sciences. It is important to support research in the humanities, the first page of this document declared, because after all such research feeds directly into the tourist and heritage 'industries' which in turn fill the national coffers with so many millions per year. This is, of course, seen as the shrewdly pragmatic case necessary to persuade politicians to agree to spend the money, since politicians are supposed to be endlessly trying to second-guess the likely responses of that always irascible demon-figure, the taxpayer. For all I know, these *are* the terms in which the relevant Minister justifies his annual budget to the Chancellor of the Exchequer: 'You have to remember, Chancellor, that universities aren't simply a waste of money. They, er, they, well, they keep us economically competitive and attract a lot of tourists.' 'Oh well, that's all right then, Minister for Universities, here's your dosh.'

But there is obviously something lacking in our public discourse if the only acceptable justification for spending money is that it contributes to making more money. Clearly, we need to start from somewhere else.

II

Most of the important human activities are a mixture of what we might call (using for the moment a rough and ready distinction) 'instrumental' goods and 'intrinsic' goods. That's to say, the activities are valuable to us partly because of what else they enable us to do and partly as ends in themselves. Things aren't always that clear-cut, of course, and there's a lot more that can be said about this distinction. But for the present it points well enough to the two different idioms or registers in which we need to couch the justification of the activities carried on in universities. The danger is that if we have a public discourse which can *only* accommodate the idea of instrumental goods, then we not only find it hard to justify things which are largely intrinsic goods, but we even find ourselves starting to think about them as though they were instrumental goods. And that is obviously self-defeating in the long run. After all, each chain of instrumental reasoning has to stop somewhere, when there is no further instrumental answer to the question: 'And what is *that* good for?'

Beyond a certain level of competence in literacy, numeracy, and so on, education is an activity in which the proportion of intrinsic good is relatively high. If we say that the goal of a given activity is 'to enable human beings to flourish and to exercise their capacities', it doesn't make much sense to press on and say: 'Yes, but what is *that* good for?' It may, of course, be that *philosophers* would want to press on and ask that kind of question, since one definition of philosophy might be that philosophy is that form of enquiry in which no question can be ruled out as inappropriate in advance. However, general political and cultural debate, unlike philosophy, necessarily has to take certain categories for granted, and that includes the category of some things being intrinsic goods. But we have become uncomfortable with, or suspicious of, the language of intrinsic goods, and so we tend to think that a particular case is strengthened if we can go on to say: 'And such activities are after all valuable because they increase our economic competitiveness,' though the truth is that this slides us all the way down to the bottom of the snake of instrumental reasoning again.

Commercial businesses, in this respect unlike universities, are almost entirely about instrumental goods. The return on capital is their governing criterion, and quite properly so. If the chairman of Wunder Widgets plc reported to his shareholders that it was indeed a bit of a pity that losses were so high this year, but what really mattered was that all the employees had been completely absorbed in reading Nietzsche, he'd soon be an ex-chairman. Moreover, because the goal of a business is quantitative, it can be measured. You can set a target of so many widgets produced per day at such and such a cost, and then you can measure whether this target is or isn't being met. But because most of the important goals of a university are not quantitative, they can't be measured; they will need, as I've already suggested, to be judged.

This can be a difficult notion for people to accept. We tend these days to be highly suspicious of the notion of judgement, fearing that it too easily masks prejudice, snobbery, or even favouritism. By contrast, we trust measurement because it seems to be public, objective, and even democratic. But the trouble is, as I've already insisted, that not everything that counts can be counted. Sometimes we can only know if something is a good example of its kind by the view taken of it in the long term by those competent to judge.

Take, for example, the not very contentious question: was Socrates an important philosopher? I don't believe that the average ancient Athenian taxpayer was in a position to give much of an answer to this question. And if, in order to try to ensure that their drachmas didn't go to support any of your common-or-garden third-rate philosophers, the ancient Athenians had instituted a Research Assessment Exercise of the kind now applied to universities in this country, then poor old Socrates would have had to have been classified as 'not research active'. Good teacher, mind you, the odd sexual harassment charge aside, but there's no measurable evidence of whether he was a good philosopher because he never did get round to putting reed pen to papyrus. So, founder of Western philosophy or not, he would obviously need to be persuaded to take early retirement – which is, I suppose, more or less what did happen to him.

Actually, the ancient Athenians talked of 'citizens' rather than 'taxpayers', which in itself tended to make for a better class of discussion. But they were also not so likely to make the common contemporary mistake of confusing accountability with judgement. A process of external scrutiny can determine whether the money allocated for research has indeed been spent on research, or whether instead a particular department blew it all on a staff outing to EuroDisney followed by an extravagant meal at a Paris restaurant. *That* is accountability. But such a process of external scrutiny cannot really determine whether any of the members of that department are thinking valuable thoughts. In the long run, the answer to *that* question will be found in the extent to which the thinking of people in the same field turns out to have been significantly influenced and inspired by those thoughts. In the meantime, appointments and promotions committees have to back their informed expert judgement that a particular individual is, or is likely to become, a valuable and fruitful member of a scholarly community, and then allow them to get on with it. On that basis, I'd certainly give Socrates a job, though I can't say I'd look forward to trying to interview him.

Another problem arising out of the analogy I'm discussing is that businesses which make a similar product are necessarily in competition with each other. But this is only true in a metaphorical sense for universities; scholarship is in fact an inherently *cooperative* enterprise. The problem was brought home to me when, some time ago, I received a letter from a younger scholar at another university. She had responded to something I had published by very brilliantly transposing its categories to a quite different body of material altogether. She asked whether I thought this idea worked, and if I could suggest where she might look for further evidence, and so on. I thought her suggestion likely to be a very fertile one indeed, and I gave her what little help I could. But by so doing have I scored an own goal? If she turns this, as I hope she will, into a published essay or book of her own, will I have played some small part in helping a rival outfit get a better 'rating'? If I worked in, say, an advertising agency, I bet I wouldn't even consider giving away some of my best ideas to an employee of a rival firm. But that's my point: universities are not in fact rival firms because they're not 'firms' in the first place.

And this brings me back to that 'mission statement' I mentioned earlier. If you think about it, it's clear that this glossy brochure is based on the model of the annual company report, with its pious waffle from the chairman of the board, the graphs of rising profits, and the photos showing how environment-friendly the company's noxious products are really. But the fact is that this model of report doesn't suit those activities which are what I have been calling 'intrinsic' or ends in themselves. You can't, in this sense, 'report' on the ways minds have been broadened or the quality of the thoughts that have been thought.

Imagine, for example, the same kind of brochure setting out the 'mission statement' for a medieval monastery. There'd no doubt be one bar graph showing the increasing number of souls prayed for per annum, and another showing the declining value of the tithe; there'd perhaps be a picture of a saintly elderly monk painstakingly illuminating a manuscript, and certainly pictures of younger monks happily planting vegetables and brewing beer; and of course there'd be a statement by the prior about the efficiency gains that had been made by starting matins earlier and ending vespers later. But wouldn't all that leave you with just the teensiest suspicion that something rather important about monasteries was being omitted or misrepresented here? I suppose that, before long, that zealous prior would have been headhunted to run the Spiritual Quality Assurance Agency (which would presumably have been the official name in this country for the Inquisition). Come to think of it, perhaps there are *some* analogies which aren't so misleading after all.

III

Something similar applies in attempts to justify a university education in terms of 'skills'. I recall, some time ago, hearing a revealing comment by the then head of the Quality Assurance Agency. (That was the agency set up to, er, assure quality, i.e. the body whose task it was to make sure that what was being assured was quality, or in other words, if what you wanted to do to quality was to assure it, then this was the agency for you.) He was talking about the value of studying supposedly 'useless' subjects in the humanities, and arguing that people in universities were very bad at doing the PR necessary to justify that study to the wider public. (Just in passing, one might perhaps wonder, when over 40% of the age cohort, soon to rise to 50%, pursue higher education, just who this sceptical 'public' is supposed to be made up of, but that's another question.) As an example of how much more persuasively the case *could* be presented, he said that if you tell the managing director of, in his words, 'a Birmingham metal-bashing company' that your graduates have studied medieval history, he won't be interested in recruiting them. But if you tell him that they have spent three years honing the skills necessary to arrive at sound conclusions on the basis of insufficient evidence, then he'll look upon them altogether more favourably.

My first reaction on hearing this was to reflect that I have an altogether higher estimate of the intelligence of our leading industrialists. For one thing, they already have a pretty good idea what's involved in doing medieval history, especially since many of them seem to spend their spare time reading history books anyway. But more than that, I couldn't imagine them, if they're any good at their jobs, being taken in by such a transparent piece of re-packaging. The classics graduate can, of course, *say* to the computer manufacturer that she or he hasn't actually been spending all that time studying Latin verse but has rather been 'analysing the economic encoding of meaning in units of randomly ordered noise'. But the air would surely soon be full of the sound of bells as they were invited to pull the other one. In this respect, the QAA official's remark seems a classic example of the tail wagging the dog. Our spokesman was working backwards from one description of what employers might be thought to need, and then trying to make that the justification of an activity which is actually pursued for quite other reasons.

There are, needless to say, other ways to respond to that particular example. The first, and perhaps the most radical, would be to say that it may be a mistake to try to persuade the Birmingham industrialist to employ the medieval history graduate at all. The graduate may not be the kind of employee the firm wants, and the firm may not be the kind of employment the graduate wants. Someone who chose to do medieval history in the first place may have been signalling a different set of inclinations, and so they might well, if you'll forgive my using the technical language of engineering for a moment, prove to be a square peg in a round hole.

Secondly, if those *are* the 'skills' which the firm wants, then wouldn't they be more usefully developed by working on the relevant sort of problems from the start? Trying to decide what the demand is likely to be for a new widget may have *something* in common with trying to reconstruct a history of farming practices from thirteenth-century manorial records, but it does seem an awfully roundabout route. Business schools, through their simulated case-studies approach, are good at preparing people to make such managerial decisions, so it seems a bit improbable that it would be on those grounds that the Birmingham industrialist would prefer to employ the medieval history graduate.

The truth is that, in Britain at least, one of the main reasons why employers are keen to recruit arts graduates is not to do with 'skills' at all, but because they know that these are the kinds of subjects many of the cleverest students choose to study. A lot of bright 18-year-olds find courses in history or English more interesting than courses in marketing or manufacturing, and employers also know that spending three years in the company of other clever people studying something that is intrinsically interesting and challenging certainly doesn't reduce those students' native intelligence. That's the main reason why recruiting from the upper reaches of the arts graduate population in this country is likely to net an employer a lot of the clever, lively, creative types of people any organization needs. Those employers also know that such graduates are likely to be able to see issues in a very broad perspective, and that in the long run that will be more valuable for the progress of their businesses than any number of specialist skills.

Of course, the question which the head of the Quality Assurance Agency, like similar spokesmen, was at least implicitly responding to is: why should society pay for it or at least subsidize it? Well, to begin once again with a somewhat radical thought, we might ask why equipping students for a job in the widget company (assuming for the sake of the argument that it actually did this) should automatically count as a good justification. Why should society pay to train up that employer's future workforce? Why is the money better spent just because an industrialist calculates that a graduate who has been so educated will help his firm to increase its profits than if we said it was spent on enlarging one person's understanding of human history? After all, we could equally well say that if the 'skills' involved in the two activities are supposedly so similar, we surely ought to subsidize a lot of 18-year-olds to spend three years working in a Birmingham metal-bashing factory so that they may go on to become better medieval historians. My point here is not that the student's years of study make no difference – of course they make a difference. My point is, rather, first, that the difference that is made is not best described in terms of the acquisition of 'skills'; and, second, that the justification for the activity is not to be looked for in how those supposed skills may be what a particular kind of employer is looking for.

This is all part of the larger problem of explaining and justifying what universities do, especially in the humanities. At several points in recent years my colleagues and I have been faced with a long questionnaire asking us to itemize the 'transferable skills' that students acquire as a result of studying English literature or history or similar subjects. It didn't at first seem clear what *kind* of answer was wanted, but it turned out (we were given a helpful crib sheet) that we were supposed to enter things such as 'the ability to analyse a problem into its component parts' and 'the capacity to organize a wide range of information into an intelligible order', and so on. I have to say that this seemed to me a bit like saying that in becoming athletes people learn such skills as 'the capacity to take in sufficient oxygen to enable the heart-lung system to work harder' or even 'the ability rapidly to put one foot in front of the other'. This is uncomfortably reminiscent of that style of vacuous re-description satirized by Molière in which the power of opium to induce sleep is explained in terms of its 'dormitive properties'.

In such a context, skills-talk represents a failure of nerve. It is an attempt to justify an activity not in its own appropriate terms, but in terms derived from another set of categories altogether, categories drawn from the instrumental world of commerce and industry. One could illustrate the pervasive nature of the mistake by juxtaposing the following three statements:

1. 'I decided to have children because the economy of tomorrow will need an adaptable workforce.'
2. 'I like going walking in the Lake District because it boosts gross domestic revenue from tourism.'
3. 'It's good for students to read great works of literature because they acquire the skills needed to manage a widget-manufacturing company.'

And talking of literature, it's usually at about this point in the argument that an appearance is made by one of the more bizarre and exotic products of the human imagination, namely a wholly fictive place called 'the real world'. This sumptuously improbable fantasy is quite unlike the actual world you and I live in. In the actual world that we're familiar with, there are all kinds of different people doing all kinds of different things – sometimes taking pleasure in their work, sometimes expressing themselves aesthetically, sometimes falling in love, sometimes telling themselves that if they didn't laugh they'd cry, sometimes wondering what it all means, and so on. But this invented entity called 'the real world' is inhabited exclusively by hard-faced robots who devote themselves single-mindedly to the task of making money. They work and then they die. Actually, in the fictional accounts of 'the real world' that I've read, they don't ever seem to mention dying, perhaps because they're afraid that if they did it might cause the robots to stop working for a bit and to start expressing themselves, falling in love, wondering what it all means, and so on, and once that happened, of course, 'the real world' wouldn't seem so special any more, but would be just like the ordinary old world we're used to. Personally, I've never been able to take this so-called 'real world' very seriously. It's obviously the brainchild of cloistered businessmen, living in their ivory factories and out of touch with the kinds of things that matter to ordinary people like you and me. They should get out more.

The main reason, it hardly needs saying, why anyone studies medieval history, future employment prospects aside, is that it's intrinsically very interesting. In this particular case, it also happens to be part of the past of our society, and trying to imagine a society not interested in its own past would be rather like trying to imagine a person not having a memory. And that points to another of the oddities of the skills agenda: it's a bit like training people in tricks for improving their memory but without their having any past to recall. Understanding does not work like a drop-down 'dialog box': it involves reflection on the ways the newly encountered material does or doesn't fit with categories and experiences which the understander already possesses. And reflection is more, or other, than just a 'skill'.

'Transferable skills' can only ever be a by-product of doing good work, at whatever level, not its goal. And again, if we do slide into making the developing of such skills appear to be the defining purpose of our disciplines, then we again run the risk of the reply that there are surely more direct and reliable ways to do that than by having someone decipher thirteenth-century manorial records or examine the metrical patterns in Gerard Manley Hopkins' poetry. If our purpose really *is* to enable people to write good memos to their sales force, then these look like pretty funny places to start from. The many thousands of students who apply each year to read humanities subjects at university have not on the whole been persuaded to do so by being told about the skills involved: they have for the most part found certain things they have read to be interesting, and interesting in ways which are continuous with how they find other matters interesting in other areas of their lives. Our model here should perhaps be Montaigne, who famously said (following Socrates): 'to philosophize is to learn to die.' We certainly don't improve his case by saying: 'to study philosophy is to develop transferable termination-related skills.'

IV

Even when all this has been said, there are still circumstances in which I find it very difficult to explain what I do for a living. I can use the general terms well enough, of course, and say that I am an academic, and that I teach and write, mostly in the fields of literature and history. But to the genuinely enquiring questioner, let alone to the slyly scornful, this doesn't say much about what I actually *do*. Answering that question, at least for some purposes, may require shifting to a different register.

This difficulty had been brought home to me many years ago when, at my previous university, a new vice-chancellor arrived, and it was decided that he should make a series of visits to different parts of the university to see representative figures at work in the various activities carried on there. He wandered round laboratories, hovered over practicals, sat in on lectures, and so forth, but it was suggested that he should also visit one or two selected members of the arts departments in their offices (he was a distinguished physicist). I was selected to be one of these, and told that the expectation was that he would find me 'carrying on with my research'. Naturally, I brooded a good deal over just what sort of *tableau vivant* best represented this activity: should I be correcting the proofs of my latest publication, or be discussing my exciting new 'findings' with one of my colleagues, or be on the point of filling in a large grant application? Finally, I realized that if I was supposed to represent 'research in the humanities' it was clear what I ought to be doing: I ought to be sitting alone reading a book. The emblematic figure of humane scholarship is not the professor at the lectern or the would-be author at the word processor, still less the white-coated member of a research team collecting 'data' and publishing 'results'. It is the person sitting alone reading a book. In practice, the new vice-chancellor was running late, so by the time he reached my office this serene vision of the intellectual life had been replaced by that of an increasingly nervous young lecturer chewing a pencil and wishing he'd remembered to remove from his noticeboard the mildly indecent postcard he'd received from a colleague the previous summer, complete with unflattering remarks about the university's administration. But perhaps this made me more genuinely representative than my implausibly Platonic notion. In the event, the V-C proved to be even more nervous, and the time passed innocuously enough in my asking him, rather as though it were an admissions interview, why he had wanted to become a vice-chancellor.

As I have got older and more senior in rank, more and more of my time has been devoted to tasks which are neither teaching nor research, tasks which get grouped under the capacious heading of 'administration' or 'professional contribution'. In some respects, this makes it easier to give a readily intelligible answer to questions about how I pass my day; there is nothing particularly esoteric about chairing committee meetings, drafting reports, reading job or grant applications, and so on. I do not take the view, which some colleagues affect to hold, that these tasks are simply tiresome and unnecessary distractions from the 'real' business of research. As I have been trying to argue in this book, universities are organizations for the maintenance, extension, and transmission of intellectual enquiry; this is necessarily a collective enterprise and one which transcends the needs or interests of the present generation, let alone of the individual scholar. This enterprise requires, among other things, active citizenship on the part of the long-term inhabitants of the scholarly republic: no one else can make the judgements about who should be appointed to jobs or what should be taught in the syllabus or what work makes an important contribution to its field, and so on. These obligations mark one of the differences between the role of the university teacher and that of the independent scholar. There is an obligation on scholars in universities to try to hand on to their successors an intellectual and institutional inheritance that will enable enquiry to be carried on at the highest level in the future. It is the whole intangible fabric or texture of scholarship and science that needs to be sustained and improved, something that goes beyond what the current bureaucratese might call 'the infrastructure'. Still, an account of what I 'do' which was entirely comprised of such activities really would seem to be missing out the essential part of the business (though there are, sad to report, weeks for which such an account would be a wholly accurate description). So I come back to the difficulty of finding adequate representations of the experience of intellectual enquiry, at least in the literary and historical fields that most interest me.

I was put on the spot about this in a different way a few years ago. When my book *Absent Minds: Intellectuals in Britain* was about to be published in 2006, I was asked to contribute to the 'Don's Diary' feature which regularly appears in my university's alumni magazine. This led me to glance back at pieces written for this slot in earlier issues. As usual, I was impressed, and a little intimidated, by the achievements of my colleagues: the genre may seem to invite an extended solo for own trumpet, and some colleagues had not been bashful. But nonetheless I had an uneasy sense not just that I didn't recognize myself in their brightly upbeat and wearyingly energetic accounts (some of them were uncannily reminiscent of those Christmas circular letters), but that the essential activity of being a scholar or scientist, the very business of thinking and writing, was not being represented at all. At the same time, I was well aware that published scholarship quite often involves an elaborate exercise in covering one's tracks: it presents the arguments and evidence in favour of one's claims, not the chancy, indirect process by which one arrived at this position or how this fitted in to one's other activities. So when it came to my turn to contribute to the page, I decided I would try to give the reader at least some slight sense of what the working week of a scholar in the humanities was actually like. This was the result.

Don's Diary

++++ It is not easy to describe the distinctive nature of scholarship in the humanities. It can sometimes seem that the most honest entry in 'diary' form might go something like this: 'Got up even earlier; re-read what I wrote yesterday; crossed most of it out; despair; suddenly saw what I was trying to say; finally chiselled out several sentences that didn't seem too bad; jubilation.' That could count as a fairly successful morning's 'research' (at least until one read over those sentences the following morning). It can, of course, all be expressed in a quite different register, emphasizing the deepening of understanding about some of the profoundest human experiences, the increase in the clarity and exactness of our descriptions, and so on. But the slow realization of these long-term goals rarely translates into 'news'. This may help explain why we often take a somewhat jaundiced view of those university-sponsored publications that purport to describe its activities to a wider world. Such publications, when not wholly devoted to 'funding initiatives', tend to be full of items about the 'collaborative ventures' and 'exciting discoveries' of our scientific colleagues. The humanities don't tend to generate headlines in the same way: 'Cambridge scholar finally finishes draft chapter' doesn't quite cut it.

We do collaborate all the time, of course; it's just that most of our collaborators are dead. They are other scholars whom we've never met but whose work has, often long after its initial publication, stirred and fertilized our thinking (one reason why a fully stocked library is our equivalent of a state-of-the-art laboratory). And we do make discoveries, of a kind, though they more often involve seeing a whole chunk of a subject in a new way or connecting the previously unconnected rather than the literal finding out of something nobody had ever known before.

I'm stirred to these thoughts by its being publication day for my book, *Absent Minds: Intellectuals in Britain*. On good days, I've sustained myself through the long years of its composition by the thought that it deals with quite an important subject in a relatively new and illuminating way (not all days are good days). Given the labour that goes into any scholarly book, to call P-Day something of an anti-climax is wildly to overstate the excitement involved. 'Publication' often seems to mean the date by which a publisher's stock-records show that copies are being held in a warehouse deep in the country-side, so that should anyone happen, by a chance encounter with the author's mother, to learn of its existence, a copy could (theoretically) be ordered and arrive within, oh, barely four to six weeks.

However, it's all rather different on this occasion, partly because the book's topic is bound to attract a little mild curiosity from the general media, and partly because Oxford University Press have done an excellent job with the advance publicity. All of which turns out to be something of a mixed blessing . . .

++++ To Broadcasting House to take part in brief discussion of my book for Radio 3. 'So, Stefan Collini, what is an intellectual . . .?' 'So, what you're really saying is . . .' 'Well, I'm afraid that's all we have time for . . .' Aaarrrggghh.

++++ To the Royal Society of Arts to lecture and answer questions about the book. 'So, what is an intellectual . . .?' 'So, what you're really saying is . . .' 'Which celebrity would you most like to discuss this topic with . . .?' (I spontaneously reply 'Thierry Henry', then wish I'd said 'Juliet Stevenson', then realize this is all completely bonkers.)

++++ To the newsagent to buy (hoping not to be seen) copy of smart weekly which I'm told carries a review of my book. Wish I hadn't: the don-shooting season has obviously started. I paraphrase: 'Pontificat-ing academic ruined my weekend with tedious tome, the long-winded bugger; anyway, have you heard the one about the intellectual, the Irishman . . .'

++++ Home to lick wounds. Console self that the real thing, as all scholars know, is not the immediate reception of one's work, but whether it goes on to play its part in stirring the thinking of its readers, some of whom may use it to help make their own books a little bit better. When that happens, then we really do have a news headline to match all the fanfare about those 'discoveries' by our scientific colleagues: 'Cambridge scholar cited in footnote to obscure monograph.' Hold the front page.

++++ To meeting of Faculty Board where we are told that the university wants us to 'generate' more 'research income'. Successfully control my temper and express judicious-sounding reservation. But really! High-quality research in my field depends, overwhelmingly, on having time free from other distractions (plus access to aforementioned good library). Regular sabbatical leave is the key, understood not as a period in which you 'complete' a 'project', but as a space within which you start to ruminate about an unobvious question and find out whether you might, one day, have something interesting to say about it. The origin and purpose of grants and similar kinds of 'outside income' is to pay for expenses incurred in carrying out such a piece of research, so being told to *pursue* 'outside funding' amounts to the instruction: 'You must find extra ways to incur expenses'. More material for the fast-growing field of tail/dog wag-relation studies.

++++ Unfortunately, too much of my life these days seems to be spent in meetings discussing ways of supporting other people's research rather than doing any of my own. To London to chair meeting of the Modern Literature section of the British Academy: postdoctoral fellowships to be awarded, grants to be given, policies to be formulated . . . The academic profession is sustained by what is essentially voluntary labour: one of the several idiocies of the audit culture increasingly ruling universities is that it will liquidate this huge fund of good will. 'My fee for chairing a committee starts at £2,000, plus malpractice insurance premiums . . .'

++++ To the Pitt Building on Trumpington St for a meeting of the Cambridge University Press Syndicate (every second Friday afternoon in term). Get good upper-body workout just carrying the two-volume doorstopper of agenda papers. As always, am impressed by the amount of time and care many referees devote to the reports they write on typescripts the Press is considering for publication. The authors of these books are in effect getting extended postdoctoral supervisions from some of the leading authorities on their subject; it is not uncommon, after three or four closely reasoned pages of criticism and suggestion about the structure and argument of a book, to find the report abbreviated with the laconic note: '8pp of detailed comments follow'. Why do eminent, busy, scholars work so hard at this all-but-unpaid and usually anonymous task? Perhaps some sense of commitment to the discipline and of shared intellectual standards? Perhaps because in the past others did these things for us and now it's our turn?

++++ Spend Saturday morning weeding (emails, that is), writing references, and drafting minutes of Thursday's meeting. Next on the pile is a request for a report on the workings of an appointments committee of which I was an external member: this will be a completely superfluous document, demanded in the name of a misplaced notion of 'accountability'. Feel like a harassed, overworked middle manager in an underfunded company: wonder what happened to youthful dreams of intellectual excitement and literary glory. Yet as I stare out of the window across to a neighbouring faculty building and see two extremely distinguished scholars in their separate offices, at noon on a Saturday, giving their keyboards hell, I also feel some mixture of collective pride and individual luck. There *they* are, hammering out their reports and references and assessments of typescripts and so on while also, somehow, finding time to write the sort of books that (in their cases, anyway) have changed the face of scholarship. Perhaps that points to the real headline news. 'Cambridge don feels ambivalent about job but almost clears his inbox.'

8

HiEdBizUK

We see a higher education sector which meets the needs of the economy in terms of trained people, research and technology transfer. At the same time it needs to enable all suitably qualified individuals to develop their potential both intellectually and personally, and to provide the necessary storehouse of expertise in science and technology, and the arts and humanities which defines our civilization and culture.

It is hardly surprising that universities in Britain are badly demoralized. Even those statements which are clearly intended to be upbeat affirmations of their importance have a way of making you feel slightly ill. It is not simply the fact that no single institution could successfully achieve all the aims crammed into this unlovely paragraph, taken from the introductory chapter to the government's White Paper *The Future of Higher Education*, published earlier this year. It is also the thought of that room in Whitehall where these collages are assembled. As the findings from the latest survey of focus-groups come in, an official cuts out all those things which earned a positive rating and then glues them together in a straight line. When a respectable number of terms have

---

This essay was originally written late in 2003 when the proposals outlined in the White Paper (*The Future of Higher Education* [London: HMSO, 2003]) were before Parliament.

been accumulated in this way, s/he puts a dot at the end and calls it a sentence.

There are two sentences in the paragraph quoted above. The first, which is clear enough though not a thing of beauty, says that the main aim of universities is to turn out people and ideas capable of making money. The second, which is neither clear nor beautiful, says there are a lot of other points that it's traditional to mention in this connection, and that they're all good things too, in their way, and that the official with the glue-pot has been having a busy day, and that we've lost track of the subject of the verb in the last line, and that it may be time now for another full stop.

It should be acknowledged that it is not easy to characterize what universities are and what they now do, and so not easy to lay down a 'vision' of what they might do in the future. That is partly because of the intrinsic difficulty of talking about intellectual activity in terms that are both general and useful, partly because the 'higher education sector' embraces a diverse range of institutions each of which is something of a palimpsest of successive social and educational ideals. But it is also and above all because the populist language that tends to dominate so much discussion in contemporary market democracies is not well adapted to justifying public expenditure in other than economic or utilitarian terms, and it is principally as a form of expenditure – and a problematic or resented one at that – that universities now attract political and media attention. Nonetheless, this may be a particularly important moment to try to think a little harder about universities and their future than the slack, prefabricated prose of the White Paper allows, since Parliament is about to debate the proposals it contains, and it is already obvious that the legislation that ensues will have far-reaching consequences.

One must, of course, be realistic about the genre to which this document belongs. It is a functional production, doubtless the work of many hands; it is not a philosophical meditation on its subject nor does it aim at literary distinction. Nonetheless, some White Papers have in the past constituted major statements about an area of our common life, and one would at least expect the phrasing of such an important document to reflect the fact that is has been worked on intensively by some of the best minds among politicians, civil servants, policy advisers, and so on.

The alarming thought is that it may indeed reflect that process. In this respect, the whole bullet-point-riddled assemblage is an index of the difficulty which the public language of a contemporary market democracy has with social goods that can neither be quantified nor satisfactorily distributed by means of a market mechanism.

It's hard to know where to start. The issue on which the present government has its knickers most completely in a twist is 'access', and, not surprisingly, there is a whole chapter in the White Paper devoted to 'Fair Access'. Every year a large part of the media coverage of universities concerns this issue, too, with vacuous stories about some school pupil from a working-class background who is rejected by snobby Oxbridge despite getting outstanding A-levels. The general implication of these stories is that, in an otherwise fair and open society, elitist universities continue to favour the offspring of the traditionally privileged.

So, to restore a little sanity to this issue, let's begin with the following, rather striking, fact. In Britain, entrance to a university is almost the only widely desired social good that cannot be straightforwardly bought. Money can buy you a better house than other people; money can buy you better health care; money can even buy you a better school education for your children. In each of these cases it is a simple cash transaction. Our society apparently feels no shame about any of this: advertisements in the national media spell out in the starkest terms the advantages your child will get, including the improved exam results, if you can afford the high school fees. But money cannot directly buy you a better university place for your child, or indeed a place at all (apart from at the private University of Buckingham, whose recruitment pattern confirms that it has not become the institution of choice for most British students). Of course, as in any strongly class-divided society, advantages are self-perpetuating: statistically, children of the wealthy stand a much better chance of going to university than do children of the poor (interestingly, children of the well-educated stand a better chance still). But the facts are the very reverse of the picture painted by silly-season newspaper headlines: money can buy you pretty much everything except love and university entrance.

The whole question of 'access', therefore, needs to start from somewhere else. It is absurd to think that universities can unilaterally correct for the effects of a class-divided society. Of course the figures showing how much greater are the chances of children of the professional classes going to university than children of manual workers reveal a scandalous situation. But the scandal is not about university admissions; it is about the effect of social class in determining life-chances; the corresponding figures about, say, mortality are a much worse scandal.

As with so many other matters in contemporary public debate, serious thinking about class has been displaced by shallow sloganeering about 'elitism'. One of the reasons the admission-season stories can be worked up in the way that they are is because the individual cases can be made to seem to turn on adventitious matters like accent or manners. Anything which smacks of favouring what were the contingent accoutrements of the dominant class in an earlier period are 'outmoded', 'archaic', 'elitist' (the stories are usually accompanied by Bridesheady images of supposed Oxbridge types in dinner jackets and punts). The outrage is that a working-class girl from, say, Essex or Tyneside is being 'dissed'. Clubby upper-class men are cloning themselves, admitting chaps who 'fit in', and so on.

Now, it goes without saying that the judgements of university admissions tutors are fallible, but as an account of systematic bias currently at work in the process this fantasy doesn't stand up to a moment's scrutiny. One wonders whether the journalists who write these stories have ever met any contemporary admissions tutors or considered their, often far from privileged, social backgrounds – or even noticed the fact that a lot of them are not male. And one also has to ask what the academics' motives are supposed to be for selecting less able Hooray Henrys to have to teach for the next three years. For the most part, university teachers have a much more real and informed interest in the intellectual 'potential' of those whom they are to teach than do the mouthy hordes of journalists and politicians over-quick to scent scandal. The majority of these stories are in any case based on the misleading premise that very good A-level results will guarantee applicants entry to the university of their choice, when in fact top universities could often fill their places many times over with applicants who have such results, so that other factors, including judgements about intellectual autonomy and suitability for the course, legitimately come into play. The willingness of leading members of the government to sound off about the shameful 'elitism' they insist must have informed such judgements only shows how quick they are to attack what they think will be soft targets with populist appeal. This is the other face of 'modernization': we need to sweep away 'privilege' in the form of the trappings of status, but we allow the market to entrench the real differentials of class more deeply than ever.

In these circumstances it would take an exceptionally clear-headed and brave official document on higher education not to succumb to making cheap shots about 'access', and it will already be clear how far this White Paper is from displaying those qualities. Of course, some of what it says about 'opportunity' and 'potential' and so on is unexceptionable enough, and to its credit it does acknowledge that the story starts much further back, with matters of family background and early schooling. But it never seems to grasp the full significance of this acknowledgement nor to understand how, in consequence, participation rates for different social groups are only marginally affected by variations in universities' admissions practices. This obtuseness is particularly evident when the White Paper observes, almost in passing: 'It is worth noting that students from lower socio-economic groups who do achieve good A-levels are as likely to go on to university as young people from better-off backgrounds.' The sentence isn't sufficiently precise in its phrasing really to do the work that it promises – do the young people from better-off backgrounds have the *same* results, do they go to the *same* universities? – but it surely makes clear enough that the problem is not to do with university admissions in themselves. Nonetheless, the White Paper pushes on in the only way it knows how: by setting 'benchmarks' for each institution to achieve in recruiting from 'low-participation groups', and then setting 'improvement targets for year-on-year progress'. And what if admissions officers find that not enough schoolchildren with 'potential' apply from the right postcodes (or whatever other rough marker of 'disadvantage' is used)? Tough: they'll fail to meet their 'targets', and their institutions' funding will suffer accordingly. It seems possible that the early stages of consultation have led the government to drop or modify the idea of an

'Access Regulator' who would check that individual universities were meeting their access 'contract', and would deny them the right to charge higher fees if they weren't. But the fundamental confusion remains.

A still deeper confusion is at work in the signs of the off-the-cuff manpower planning that informs this document. Its premise, as we have seen, is that higher education needs 'to enable all suitably quali- fied individuals to develop their potential'. But how many people is this, and how can we know? You may well think it is impossible to answer that question, and you'd be right. But the government knows. Or at least it knows, apparently, that by 2010 50% of the age cohort in this country will have the potential to develop themselves intellectu- ally and personally in higher education. The absurdity of this marriage of high principle and random guesswork becomes more glaring a few pages later when we are told in successive bullet points that

> our vision is of a sector which:
> - offers the opportunity of higher education to all those who have the potential to benefit
> - is expanding towards 50 per cent participation for young people 18–30 years from all social backgrounds.

There is clearly a case for trying to extend the Geneva Convention to outlaw the dumb-dumb bullet-point as a particularly inhumane form of intellectual warfare. The obvious fact is that the '50% in higher edu- cation' was an opportunist soundbite, a figure chosen for its electoral appeal, not as the expression of some deep analysis of the population's intellectual potential, still less of an understanding of the nature of uni- versity education. Most of that expansion, entirely reasonably, will not take place in traditional university courses anyway. Much of it will be in directly vocational and employment-directed forms of training, and some may happen within a proposed two-year 'foundation degree'. These are good and necessary things for the state to help to provide, but there is no rational way to determine how many people, short of the entire population, should benefit from them.

A similar incoherence is evident in the chapter ominously entitled 'Teaching and Learning – Delivering Excellence', which speaks of 'all' students having the right to choose the 'best' places. 'All students are entitled to high-quality teaching' and to the information that will enable them to choose where to study. Publishing information about teaching quality will, through the operation of consumer choice, 'drive up quality'. Students need this information in order, as the White Paper unashamedly puts it, 'to become intelligent customers of an increasingly diverse provision' (Cardinal Newman, thou shou'dst be living at this hour!). But if teaching in some places is better than in others, then, logically, not 'all' students can have access to it. Ah, but 'student choice will increasingly work to drive up quality', so before long everywhere will be 'best'. Standards will be 'high and continually improved'. What do they think they mean by 'continually improved'? This is advertisers' pap, but teaching isn't soap powder. What kind of 'right' to choose the best place is being exercised when everywhere is, in this performance-indicator sense, 'best'? And should we all simply acquiesce in the blithe assumption about consumer choice 'driving up standards' – as it has done in the case of, say, TV programmes or the railways?

Ironically, the White Paper itself illustrates the logical problem here in its comments on 'measuring student achievement'. It worries about the 'increasing numbers of first- and upper-second-class degrees' and wants to look at alternative methods of measuring student achievement. But this is exactly the problem inherent in all attempts to combine measurement (rather than judgement) with targets, benchmarks, league tables, and all the other paraphernalia of market simulation. You devise some system which supposedly measures achievement in quantitative terms and you allocate rewards on the basis of these scores; you decree that more of the players (universities, schools, individuals) have to exceed a certain score; then when they inevitably do so, you cry that the currency has been debased and you have to start again from somewhere else.

II

The prize for bare-faced inanity goes, perhaps predictably, to the White Paper's comment on the Research Assessment Exercise (RAE), which has been carried out every five years since its introduction in 1986. It proclaims that the RAE 'has undoubtedly led to an overall increase in quality over the last fifteen years'. Rarely can the Fallacy of the Self-Fulfilling Measurement System have been better illustrated. More departments receive higher ratings now than in 1986 when the system was instituted: ergo, quality has gone up. This corresponds to the period assessed by RAEs: ergo, it is the existence of the RAEs that have 'led to' this 'increase in quality'. In reality, it is hard to see how anyone could *know* whether there had been some general 'increase in quality' in the research and scholarship carried on across all subjects in all British universities during this period. What can be said is that the RAE is a crude form of measurement that is used to distribute funds to universities: its indisputable effect has been to encourage academics to publish more, and more quickly. It is not obvious, let alone indisputable, that this situation has been conducive to any 'increase in quality'.

There are moments, it has to be said, when one starts to wonder whether the officials at the Department for Education and Skills aren't indulging in their own little joke. For example, as part of the policy of encouraging excellence in teaching (can there be a kind of policy that doesn't do this?), a few university departments will be designated 'Centres of Teaching Excellence' and given all kinds of goodies. But then (don't laugh), in order to recognize those departments that come close, but not quite close enough, to this standard, the Higher Education Funding Council for England (HEFCE) 'will also offer a "commended" status'. This will 'make it clear to prospective students that they can expect a particularly high standard of teaching on their course'. We have now entered the world of hotel and restaurant guides: some departments will have signs next to the entrance saying 'HEFCE commended', while prospective students will decide whether they will be content with 'plain regional teaching' (one mortar-board), or would prefer 'high-quality teaching in its category' (two mortar-boards), or perhaps even stretch to 'exceptional teaching of international quality' (three mortar-boards). Suicides among heads of departments who are stripped of one of the coveted mortar-boards cannot be ruled out.

One of the most predictable places where pseudo-market guff comes in is the issue of 'rewards' for academics (as if they had just found lost treasure or an escaped criminal). HEFCE has already been on to this, we are told, with its insistence that certain elements of the annual grant are tied to institutions having in place 'human-resources strategies' which, above all, 'reward good performance': 'This process has successfully kick-started the modernization of human-resource management in higher education.' 'Modernization' is, of course, trademark NewLabourSpeak, here combined with the language of the personnel departments of commercial companies. What it essentially means is that, given a number of people doing roughly the same job, a way has to be found to pay some of them less than others. Otherwise, given the assumptions of market democracy, no one will have sufficient reason to try to do their best: they will only do this if they can see that it could earn them more money than their colleagues. 'Modern' here means using the market model. Result: endless procedures involving specious attempts to measure effort or effectiveness which have the net effect of being divisive and demoralizing. On this point it is worth recalling the moral confidence of what one historian has described as 'one of the great state papers of this century', the Robbins Report of 1963: 'We believe any such disparity between the incomes and prospects of persons doing similar work in different universities, which are all in receipt of public funds, to be unjust; and we consider its effects to be harmful.'

How remote that seems from the idiom of management consultancy in which these matters are discussed now. 'Comparing US and UK academic salaries, it is striking that the difference in average salary scales is far smaller than the difference in salaries at the top end for the best researchers. This raises questions about whether our institutions are using salaries to the best possible effect in recruiting and retaining excellent researchers.' Does it? Or does it suggest that Fat Cat Syndrome is not yet as out of hand in British as in some American universities? It is another of the misplaced market assumptions of our time that giving a lot of money to a few individuals at the top of an institution is what best contributes to the overall performance of that institution. In fact, in many activities morale, commitment, cooperation, and a sense of solidarity are far more precious, and they tend to be fostered by a system that uses only modestly differentiated pay scales.

More generally, the language of the White Paper repeatedly reveals that the only terms in which the government believes the electorate can be conned into supporting universities are those of economic gain. The madness that follows from this is most starkly evident in, yet again, the discussion of 'participation rates'. It is worth observing that, as historians of education have constantly demonstrated, all measures of participation in higher education are controversial and depend upon contested definitions; hence the pitfalls in drawing conclusions from what may not be properly comparable data. For example, according to OECD figures, Poland has a 62% net entry rate for first degree or equivalent education, whereas Germany has only 30%, which doubtless accounts for the fabled superiority in economic performance of Poland over Germany . . . But let's accept for the moment that in Britain the rate has gone up from something like 6–8% of the age cohort in the early 1960s to something like 43–44% today. The White Paper is keen to disarm possible criticisms of this trend, and so it goes on: 'Despite the rise in numbers participating in higher education, the average salary premium has not declined over time and remains the highest in the OECD. It is not the case that "more means worse".' So that's what Kingsley Amis and the Black Paper critics were really on about: letting in the hoi polloi might endanger earnings differentials. The crassness of the thinking here hardly needs comment: it's all right for you to be allowed to go to university – as long as it still leads to your earning more than certain other people.

But notice, too, the picture of society that is implied in this unlovely argument. When only 6% of the age cohort went to universities, they went on to earn on average (let us say) twice what the members of the remaining 94% earned. Now 43% of the age cohort go to university and each of them also earns twice what members of the remaining 57% do. What this actually points to is a marked, though still limited, diffusion of prosperity and a radically changing social and occupational structure. Thus, it is entirely possible, given the social and economic changes of the past fifty years, that the same 43% would be earning twice as much as their less fortunate brethren even if universities didn't exist. Still, there is a glimpse here of one possible criterion this government may be working with to decide at what level to cap 'participation' in higher education: there have to be enough people outside to look down on in order to make the whole business of becoming a graduate worthwhile.

The question of whether these higher salaries are actually the result of their recipients having had a university education also exposes the fatuity of the rhetoric of 'potential' and 'fairness'. Let us, first of all, attend honestly to the facts of who gets a higher education. Overwhelmingly, it is the children of the professional and middle classes, who come from homes which give them cultural and linguistic advantages from an early age, which help them to succeed at school, which develop their educational and career aspirations, and so on. In formal terms, those who go to universities are on the whole those who, largely for these kinds of reason, get the best results in the school-leaving examination system. Now let's suppose there were no such institutions as universities, and everybody went straight into work at age 18 or 19. Who would be likely to be earning, on average, salaries twice those of their contemporaries? Exactly the same people as do so now. Charging universities with 'elitism' because they are largely powerless to dent this structure of systematic injustice is a particularly telling indication of the extent to which this government has come to endorse a version of the familiar American combination of market individualism plus the rhetoric of 'equal respect' plus the fail-safe of litigation.

In other ways, too, the world as imagined by this White Paper is a world of educational Darwinism. Higher education in this country is locked in mortal combat with its 'competitors' elsewhere; only the 'strongest' departments deserve proper research funding; universities 'compete' for the 'best researchers'; institutions which fail to 'price' their courses appropriately for their 'market' will be eliminated, and so on. The document urges us to wise up to these realities: 'Our competitors are looking to sell higher education overseas, into the markets we have traditionally seen as ours.' This may indeed reflect the practice of some universities, but may there not be a distinction between 'attracting good students from overseas' and 'selling higher education' in those 'markets'? And might that distinction not rest on the difference between deepening international links in a common transnational intellectual enquiry on the one hand and making a profit on the other?

Indeed, in what relevant sense *are* other countries 'our competitors' where intellectual activities are concerned? This bit of market language has become so pervasive that we hardly notice it any more. What chiefly lies behind it is an assumption about who reaps the economic benefits of applied science. But it is not clear that this is any kind of zero-sum game: the benefits brought by the widespread use of any particular form of technology across a wide range of societies far outweigh any notional benefit to the country in which a certain stage or application of the relevant science was first developed. And anyway, applied technology is not the whole or even the greater part of what universities do – at least, not yet. There may be *rivalry* between different national groups of scholars as between individuals, but not in any meaningful sense *competition*. British archaeologists are enriched not impoverished if one of their colleagues from another country unearths a key bit of the jigsaw of an ancient civilization.

But then scholarship of this kind, scholarship in the humanities that may be undertaken by individuals but which relies upon and contributes to cumulative intellectual enquiry which transcends boundaries between nations as well as between generations and which has little direct economic utility, scarcely figures in the White Paper, so preoccupied is it with science seen as a source of technological applications. About a third of the way into the chapter on 'Research Excellence – Building On Our Strengths' there is one numbered paragraph that consists only of a single short sentence. Its combination of intellectual flaccidity and lazy off-handedness is at once breathtaking and depressing. In its entirety it reads: '2.10: Some of these points are equally valid for the arts and humanities as for science and technology.'

III

In political terms, the two hottest potatoes among the government's proposals concern fees and their payment by students. The plan is, first, to allow universities to choose whether or not to introduce 'top-up fees', up to a limit presently set at £3,000, over and above the existing system-wide fees. The assumption seems to be that the leading universities, confident that they would still attract the best students, would choose to charge the additional fees, while less-well-placed institutions might opt to 'compete on price' by not doing so. The second element in the proposal is then to 'charge' these fees to the students concerned, though not as up-front payments but as a form of tax levied on their subsequent earnings. These two proposals are presented as part of a single package, but they could in fact be decoupled. Requiring students to contribute individually to the costs of their university education does not entail the divisive and inadequate notion of 'top-up fees': it could perfectly well be combined with the abolition of 'fees', which are anyway a partly symbolic notation for a contract that is made directly between universities and the government, replacing them with a simple increase in direct funding. Under the proposed 'Graduate Contribution Scheme', which is clearly preferable to the present regime of up-front fees, the state would in time recoup much of this outlay without introducing a financially distorted 'market' among universities and courses.

According to the proposed scheme, once graduates start to earn beyond a certain limit (£15,000 is suggested for the first year of the scheme), a small amount is deducted from their earnings through the tax system up to a point where they are considered to have 'repaid' a contribution to the costs of the education that they were publicly subsidized to undertake at the time. But the justification given for this measure runs together two different principles: that of students paying 'the cost of the course', and that of students paying in some proportion to their later earnings. Although in some cases (e.g. medicine) these principles might point in the same direction, they certainly will not do so in general, and it ought to be clear that the second is a more acceptable basis than the first. Students should not have to pay individually for education: that is a public good whose costs one generation of the community defrays for the next. But insofar as prospective higher earnings are either a motive to undertake higher education or a consequence of it, then there is an argument for saying that students should contribute in proportion to the benefit gained (though the actual proposal is for a flat-rate, not a graduated, tax). But the idea of students paying the 'cost of the course' is one of the places where the whole commercial language of students as customers making price-sensitive purchases is so misleading.

Any calculation of the 'cost' of a university 'course' is pretty notional anyway. So much goes on at a university that is not specific to any particular course that it's next to impossible to work out the real 'costs' spent on each student (as opposed to some arbitrary percentage of existing departmental budgets and so on). And in any event the 'cost of the course' principle has potentially pernicious consequences: no one with a vocation to do so should be deterred from studying medicine because the fees are higher, any more than someone should unenthusiastically enrol for a philosophy degree because it's cheap. Ever since 'Blunkett's botch' in 1998, when the then Secretary of State for Education, in the face of expert advice to the contrary, opted to introduce fees, payable by students in advance, and to phase out maintenance grants, the government has been struggling, and failing, to combine the aims of widening 'access', forcing students to make a higher direct contribution to the costs of their education, and providing universities with adequate yet politically acceptable levels of funding. A suitably long-term form of the 'Graduate Contribution Scheme' would be one of the least damaging ways to achieve these goals, 'top-up fees' one of the most damaging.

Although the White Paper contains some proposals that may be welcomed, it is hard to see the panicky bravado evident in so much of its language ultimately helping to do anything but further demoralize universities in this country. Which is not to say that we should be trying to go back to some status quo ante, even if there were any agreement on when, exactly, that was. But it would be a good start to acknowledge that the diverse activities now carried on in institutions called 'universities' may require justification in diverse terms. In principle, this should be done in a way that makes clear that 'different' does not mean 'inferior', but in practice cultural attitudes may be too deeply entrenched. Just as a kind of snobbery helped to sink the idea of the polytechnics in the end, so snobbery, and the anxieties snobbery expresses, may be the biggest obstacle to trying once again to differentiate types of institution in terms of their respective functions. It would also help if proper acknowledgement were made of the fact that the social patterns legible in the statistics about who goes to university are largely determined by forces beyond universities' own admissions practices. It may be that the outdated perceptions about universities that fuel public suspicion about admissions will diminish as we approach the point where half the adult population comes to experience higher education at first hand (though that experience may, of course, foster other resentments). In that case, provided that a broadly satisfactory system of funding is put in place (a large and perhaps optimistic assumption), then it seems possible that, while there will no doubt always be individuals who feel they have been unjustly rejected by a university of their choice, there will be less political mileage to be made out of such cases in the name of 'access'.

What is more doubtful is whether any government will have the political courage to declare a university education a social good, the costs of which each generation helps to bear for its successors. This would involve acknowledging the limits of justifications couched exclusively in terms of increased economic prosperity. It might involve acknowledging that a university education (as opposed to other kinds of post-school training or professional preparation) may not be appropriate and desirable for everyone, and may anyway not be something the state can now fund on a universal basis. And, perhaps more difficult still, it would involve accepting that there are some kinds of intellectual enquiry that are goods in themselves, that need to be pursued at the highest level, and that will almost certainly continue to require a certain amount of public support. These may now form a relatively minor part of the activities carried on in universities, and it is much easier, using economic and utilitarian arguments, to justify the other activities; but they remain indispensable. Amid the uncertainties currently facing universities, the only certain thing is that these are all problems which will be exacerbated rather than solved by placing them in the lap of a deity called 'the market'.

9
Impact

I

What follows is, I assure you, neither a satire nor a parody, though I suppose it might seem laughable were it not so serious.

For more than two decades, the distribution of that element in the funding of British universities that supports research has been determined by the outcome of successive 'Research Assessment Exercises' (RAEs). These have, roughly speaking, required all university departments to submit evidence of their research over the relevant period (usually five years). The evidence has chiefly consisted of a number of publications per member of staff, plus information about the 'research environment' of the department (measures for encouraging and supporting research, including for PhD students) and evidence of 'esteem' (forms of scholarly recognition, professional roles and honours). All this material has been assessed by panels of senior academics covering particular disciplines or groups of cognate disciplines, with 'scores' awarded on the basis of a fairly simple formula, greatest weight being given to the quality of the submitted publications. The highest-scoring

---

Research Excellence Framework: Second Consultation on the Assessment and Funding of Research (London: HEFCE, 2009). This 'consultation' document invited responses before its December deadline; my article was originally published in November 2009.

departments then receive a greater share of the funding; inevitably, the scores are also used to generate league tables.

In practice, the exercise has been flawed in various obvious ways as well as hugely time-consuming. In response to cumulative criticism, the government announced a couple of years ago that it was considering discontinuing the exercise or replacing it with something much simpler. In the event, it was decided that no better way to determine the distribution of this funding could be found, and so the exercise would have to carry on, albeit in modified form. To save face, the new form was re-named the Research Excellence Framework (REF). The guidelines spelling out how it will operate have just been issued by the Higher Education Funding Council for England (HEFCE). The document declares that certain aspects of the process have yet to be settled, and so it invites responses from universities (and other interested parties) during a brief 'consultation period'.

In many respects, the REF will be quite like the RAE, and will require similar kinds of evidence in the submissions (selected publications, information about research environment, etc.). But one very significant new element has been introduced. In this exercise, approximately 25% of the rating (the exact proportion is yet to be confirmed) will be allocated for 'impact'. The premise is that research must 'achieve demonstrable benefits to the wider economy and society'. The guidelines make clear that 'impact' does *not* include 'intellectual influence' on the work of other scholars and does *not* include influence on the 'content' of teaching. It has to be impact which is 'outside' academia, on other 'research users' (and assessment panels will now include, alongside senior academics, 'a wider range of users'). Moreover, this impact must be the outcome of a university department's own 'efforts to exploit or apply the research findings': it cannot claim credit for the ways other people may happen to have made use of those 'findings'.

As always, the reality behind the abstractions which make up the main guidelines emerges more clearly from the illustrative details. The paragraphs about 'impact indicators' give some sense of what is involved. The document specifies that some indicators relate to 'outcomes (for example, improved health outcomes or growth in business revenue)'; other indicators show that the research in question 'has value to user communities (such as research income)'; while still others provide 'clear evidence of progress towards positive outcomes (such as the take-up or application of new products, policy advice, medical interventions, and so on)'. The document offers a 'menu' of 'impact indicators' that will be accepted: it runs to thirty-seven bullet points. Nearly all of these refer to 'creating new businesses', 'commercializing new products or processes', attracting 'R&D investment from global business', informing 'public policy-making' or improving 'public services', improving 'patient care or health outcomes', and improving 'social welfare, social cohesion or national security' (a particularly bizarre grouping). Only five of the bullet points are grouped under the heading 'Cultural enrichment, including improved public engagement with science and research'. These include such things as 'increased levels of public engagement with science and research (for example, as measured by surveys)' and 'changes to public attitudes to science (for example, as measured by surveys)'. The final bullet point is headed 'Other quality of life benefits': in this case, uniquely, no examples are provided. The one line of prose under this heading simply says 'Please suggest what might also be included in this list'.

The priorities indicated by these phrases recur throughout the document. For example, in explaining how the 'impact profile' of each department will be ranked as 'four star', 'three star', and so on, it provides 'draft definitions of levels for the impact sub-profiles'. That for 'three star' reads: 'highly innovative (but not quite ground-breaking) impacts such as new products or processes, relevant to several situations have been demonstrated'. (Sentence-construction is not a *forte* of the document.) And there is also a rather chilling paragraph which reads: 'Concerns have been raised about the indirect route through which research in some fields leads to social or economic impact; that is, by influencing other disciplines that are "closer to market" (for example, research in mathematics could influence engineering research that in turn has an economic impact). We intend to develop an approach that will give due credit for this.'

Clearly, the authors of this document, struggling to give expression to the will of their political masters, are chiefly thinking of economic, medical, and policy 'impacts', and they chiefly have in mind, therefore, those scientific, medical, technological, and social scientific disciplines that are, as the quoted phrase puts it, 'closer to market'. I shall not presume to speak for my colleagues in those disciplines, though I understand that they have the gravest misgivings about the distorting effect of this exercise on research in those fields. But it is a premise of the exercise that the requirements and the criteria shall be uniform across the whole span of academic disciplines (it is worth questioning why this has to be so, but I shall leave that aside for the moment), and the topic I want to address here is the potentially disastrous impact of the 'impact' requirement on the humanities.

As the phrases quoted above make clear, the guidelines explicitly exclude the kinds of impact generally considered of most immediate relevance to work in the humanities – namely, influence on the work of other scholars and influence on the content of teaching. (Those are said to be covered by the assessment of the publications themselves.) For the purposes of this part of the exercise, 'impact' means 'on research users outside universities'. General readers do not appear to count as such 'research users'. So, 25% of the assessment of the 'excellence' of research in the humanities in British universities will depend upon the evidence provided of 'impact' understood in a rather particular way. What will this mean in practice?

Let us take a hypothetical case. Let us assume that I have a col-league at another university (not all colleagues are in one's own department, despite the league-table competitiveness of these assess-ment exercises) who is a leading expert on Victorian poetry, and that over a number of years she works on a critical study of what we might call a three-star Victorian poet ('highly innovative but not quite ground-breaking'). The book is hailed by several reviewers as the best on the topic: it draws on deep familiarity not just with Victorian poetry, but with other kinds of poetry; it integrates a wealth of histor-ical and biographical learning in ways that illuminate the verse; it is exact and scrupulous in adjudicating various textual complexities; and it clarifies, modifies, and animates the understanding of this poet's work on the part of other critics and, through their writing and teaching, of future generations of students, as well as of interested general readers. It also, it is worth saying, exemplifies the general values of careful scholarship and reminds its readers of the qualities of responsiveness, judgement, and literary tact called upon by the best criticism. It is a model piece of 'excellent' research in the humanities. And its 'impact' is zero.

Of course, in any intelligent use of the word, its impact is already evident from my description of its reception, but that, as we have seen, is explicitly excluded for this purpose. Moreover, any other kind of impact is going to be credited to my colleague's department only if it can be shown to be the direct result of its own efforts. So if, say, the Departmental Impact Committee can be shown to have touted their colleague's new 'findings' to a range of producers in radio and television, and if, say, one of those producers takes an interest in this particular work, and if, say, this leads to a programme which bears some relation to the 'findings' of the book (which, if they are interesting, can probably not be summarized as 'findings' in the first place), and if, say, there is some measurable indicator of audience response to this programme, then, perhaps, the department's score will go up slightly. And if not, not.

Let us leave aside for the moment the very considerable expenditure of time and effort any such process involves (often for no result), and let us also leave aside the fact that there is no reason to expect a literary scholar to be good at this kind of hustling and hawking. There is still the fundamental question of why a department whose research happens to get taken up in this way should be any more highly rated (and rewarded) than one which does not. Not only do a variety of uncontrollable factors determine the chances of such translation to another medium, but there is also no reason to think that the success of such translation bears any relation to the research quality of the original work. If anything, meretricious and vulgarizing treatments (which concentrate on, say, the poet's sex life) may stand a greater chance of success than do nuanced critical readings. And will scholars then be encouraged to work on topics that have such 'market' potential? I recall a moment in the 1960s film *The Graduate* when a well-meaning older friend puts his hand on the young Dustin Hoffman's shoulder to give him one word of advice about a future career and whispers: 'Plastics'. Should senior scholars similarly be whispering into their junior colleagues' ears: 'Tudor monarchs'?

Not only does this exercise require all academic departments to become accomplished marketing agents; it also requires them to become implausibly penetrating and comprehensive cultural historians. For, in their submissions they will have to 'identify the research-driven contribution of the submitted unit to the successful exploitation or translation of excellent research'. Has anyone really thought about what this could involve where ideas are concerned? An experienced cultural or social historian, working on the topic for years, might – just might – be able to identify the part played by a particular piece of academic research in long-term changes in certain social practices and attitudes, but it would require a hugely detailed study and could probably only be completed long after the event and with full access to a range of types of sources. Yet every academic department is going to have to attempt something like this if they are to get any credit for the 'impact' of their 'excellent' research.

Now consider a different example. Three historians of Anglo-Saxon England, scattered across three different university history departments (there are rarely many of them in one place), read each other's work over a number of years and slowly find they are developing a revisionist view of the significance of, say, weapons found in burial hoards. They publish their findings in a series of articles in the relevant professional journals, and other scholars duly ponder and are persuaded, incorporating the new interpretation in their own writing and teaching. The curator of a regional museum, himself a recent graduate of one of these history departments who still keeps up with some of the scholarly literature, thinks that this new line would provide an excellent theme for an exhibition. He arranges for the loan of material from other museums, asks his old teacher to check the accompanying information panels, and the exhibition turns out to be very popular. This may appear to be a model case of research affecting the understanding of a wider public, but when the REF submissions are made by each of the history departments, none of this can be mentioned because the exhibition was not the direct result of the departments' own 'efforts to exploit or apply the research findings'. The impact score of the research is zero.

Adequately to capture the impact of the new 'impact' requirement on research, we probably have to pursue this example a little further. In the case of the first of the three scholars, his department's REF Committee are furious about this missed opportunity, and that scholar has to spend a considerable part of the next five years contacting museum curators and TV producers on the off-chance that his research (which he now has less time to do) will be taken up for their own purposes. He also has to produce annual reports on his efforts to do this and annual plans about his attempts to do it in the future. At the second scholar's university, a diktat comes round from the Pro-Vice-Chancellor (Research) that no funding or leave will be given to support research unless a 'demonstrable impact dimension' is in place beforehand, and staff are urged not to share with colleagues in other universities any information or contacts which might allow those universities to get in first. The second historian becomes fearful for his future: he does less research, ghost-writes the *King Alfred Book of Bread and Cake Baking*, and then becomes the university's Director of Research Strategy (Humanities). At the third university, the historian in question simply cannot stand any more of this idiocy: he takes a post at an American university and goes on to do 'highly innovative' and 'ground-breaking' (but impact-free) research which changes the way scholars all over the world think about the field.

II

We can all make half-informed guesses about how such a misconceived policy could ever have come to be imposed on British universities. Although the policy originated before the most recent Cabinet reshuffle, the fact that responsibility for higher education has now been subsumed into Lord Mandelson's Department for Business is a dispiriting indication of official attitudes. But even if universities had more powerful political champions, the truth is that the 'higher education sector' in Britain is now too large and too diverse, both in terms of types of institution and types of discipline, to be sensibly subject to a single uniform mode of assessment. The justification for the research activity of, say, a lecturer at a former polytechnic who is primarily engaged in teaching a refresher course for theatre nurses for a local health authority is bound to be different from the justification of the research activity of, say, a lecturer at a traditional university who is chiefly engaged in supervising doctoral students and teaching final-year undergraduates in Latin literature. The second may be no less valuable than the first, though in different ways, and the relations of their research to their respective publics may also be different, so those differences need to be reflected in different forms of assessment and funding.

Even if the policy represents a deliberate attempt by government to change the character of British universities (and the humanities are, I suspect, simply being flattened by a runaway tank designed for other purposes), it is still important to try to call its confusions and inade-quacies to public attention. There are, after all, some straightforward conceptual mistakes involved. For example, the exercise conflates the notions of 'impact' and of 'benefit'. It proposes no way of judging whether an impact is desirable; it assumes that if the research in ques-tion can be shown to have affected a number of people who are categorized as 'outside', then it constitutes a social benefit of that research. It also confines the notion of a 'benefit' to something that is deliberately aimed at and successfully achieved. Good work which has some wider influence without its authors having taken steps to bring this about is neither more nor less valuable than good work which has that influence as a result of such deliberate efforts, or indeed than good work which does not have that influence. And there is the obvious confusion about what is being assessed. Instead of pro-posing that 'impact' of this kind is a desirable social good over and above the quality of the research, the exercise makes the extent of such impact part of the measurement of the quality of the research. In terms of this exercise, research plus marketing is not just better than research without marketing: it is better *research*.

Underlying these tactical mistakes are larger confusions which are increasingly prevalent in public discourse. There is, to begin with, the reification of 'inside' and 'outside'. It is assumed that the only way to justify what goes on 'inside' is by demonstrating some benefit that happens 'outside'. But we are none of us wholly 'inside' or 'outside' any of the institutions or identities which partly constitute who we are; these risk becoming misleading spatial metaphors. And similarly, it is a mistake to assume that if an activity that requires expenditure (as most activities do) can be shown to have the indirect effect of also provoking expenditure by other people, then it is somehow more justified than an activity which does not have this indirect consequence. Art is a valuable human activity: showing that it also 'generates' several million pounds to the economy in terms of visits, purchases, employment, etc., does not make it a more valuable human activity.

The *OED* definition of 'impact' points to the central problem: 'The act of impinging; the striking of one body against another; collision.' In the proposed exercise, what is being sought is evidence that one body (universities) is striking against another body (not-universities, here referred to as 'society'). Nothing more than that: a mechanistic model. But the real ways in which good scholarship may affect the thinking and feeling of a wide range of people, including other scholars (who are, after all, also citizens, consumers, readers . . .), is much subtler, more long term, and more indirect than the clacking of one billiard ball against another.

It is, needless to say, perfectly proper to want specialists in any field to make an effort from time to time to explain the interest and significance of what they do to non-specialists (who may, let us remember, include specialists in other fields). Addressing such non-specialist publics is a commendable activity in itself, and it is sensible for a government, concerned about a perceived lack of public 'engagement' with academic scholarship, to wish to encourage it. But that is quite different from what is being asked for here, which is evidence of 'uptake' by 'external users' of the research itself, with such evidence (or its absence) then helping to determine the rating of the quality of that research.

I have colleagues who say that it would be a public-relations disaster for the humanities not to be subject to the same requirement of 'impact' as other disciplines, since this would lead to their being downgraded and having their funding further reduced. That the forms and criteria of impact required by this process are inappropriate to the humanities is not actually disputed by such colleagues, or by anyone else in these subjects. But they feel that the requirements are here to stay, 'consultation' period notwithstanding, and so we must all get on and 'work the system' as best we can.

There is, of course, no point in being wilfully naive about these things, but the calculated worldliness of that response may, in the long run, be self-defeating. It is not just that we should take up the challenge of 'consultation', however disingenuously that term is used, and in our responses explain as clearly as we can what is damaging about the present formulation of these guidelines. It is also that we need to try to use a more adequate language in public discussion lest these officious abstractions start to colonize our minds. One reason why measures such as these do not now provoke more vociferous opposition is that over the past three decades our sensibilities have been numbed by the proliferation of economistic officialese – the cant of 'user satisfaction', 'market forces', 'accountability', and so on. Perhaps our ears no longer hear what a fatuous, weaselly phrase 'Research Excellence Framework' actually is, or how ludicrous it is to propose that the *quality* of scholarship can be partly judged in terms of the number of 'external research users' or the range of 'impact indicators'.

Instead of letting this drivel become the only vocabulary for public discussion of these matters, it is worth insisting (as I have in Chapter 4, above) that what we call 'the humanities' are a collection of ways of encountering the record of human activity in its greatest richness and diversity. To attempt to deepen our understanding of this or that aspect of that activity is an intelligible and purposeful expression of disciplined human curiosity and is – insofar as the expression makes any sense in this context – an end in itself. Unless these guidelines are modified, scholars in British universities will devote less time and energy to this attempt, and more to becoming door-to-door salesmen for vulgarized versions of their increasingly market-oriented 'products'. It may not be too late to try to prevent this outcome.

10
Browne's Gamble

Much of the initial response to the Browne report seems to have missed the point. Its proposals have been discussed almost entirely in terms of 'a rise in fees'. Analysis has largely concentrated on the amount graduates might pay and on which social groups may gain or lose by comparison with the present system. In other words, such discussion has focused narrowly on the potential financial implications for the individual student, and here it has to be recognized that some of the details of Browne's proposed system of graduate contributions to the cost of fees are, if his premises are granted, an improvement on the present patchwork arrangements.

But the report proposes a far, far more fundamental change to the way universities are financed than is suggested by this concentration on income thresholds and repayment rates. Essentially, Browne is contending that we should no longer think of higher education as the provision of a public good, articulated through educational judgement and largely financed by public funds (albeit in recent years supplemented by a relatively small fee element). Instead, we should think of it as a lightly regulated market in which consumer demand,

---

Lord Browne et al., *Securing a Sustainable Future for Higher Education: An Independent Review of Higher Education Funding and Student Finance* (12 October 2010), www.independent.gov.uk/browne-report

in the form of student choices, is sovereign in determining what is offered by the service providers (i.e. the universities). The single most radical recommendation in the report, by quite a long way, is the almost complete withdrawal of the present annual block grant that government makes to universities to underwrite their teaching, currently around £3.9bn. This would be more than simply a 'cut', even a draconian one: it signals a re-definition of higher education and the retreat of the state from central financial responsibility for it.

Instead, Browne wants to see universities attracting customers in a competitive market-place: there will be a certain amount of public subsidy of these consumers' purchasing power, especially for those who do not go on to a reasonably well-paid job, but the mechanism which would henceforth largely determine what and how universities teach, and indeed in some cases whether they exist at all, will be consumer choice. There are, naturally, some well-meant nods towards 'assuring quality' and 'safeguarding the public interest', and it does have a few good ideas for mitigating some of the harshest financial effects of its scheme on individual students from less advantaged backgrounds. But what is of greatest significance here is not the detail of the financial arrangements but the character of the reasoning by which they are justified. Britain's universities, it is proposed, should henceforth operate in accordance with the tenets of perfect competition theory.

Nobody should pretend that all is well with British universities in their present condition. For one thing, expansion of numbers on the cheap has dramatically diluted the level of attention to individual students that most universities can provide: nearly all parents with children at university hear disturbing reports of overcrowded 'seminars' and minimal contact hours or attention to written work. In addition, there can be no doubt that the Research Assessment Exercises have, in addition to their other obvious failings, fostered a culture within universities that rewards research disproportionately more than it does teaching. The devoted university teachers of a generation or more ago who were widely read, keeping up with recent scholarship, but who were not themselves prolific publishers, have in many cases been hounded into early retirement, to be replaced (if replaced at all) by younger colleagues who see research publications as the route to promotion and esteem, and who try to limit their commitment to undergraduate teaching as far as they can.

And then there are the problems that result from trying to pretend that we have a uniform 'university system', when in fact there is a great diversity of types of institution and levels of quality. In the past two or three decades there has been a huge educational enfranchisement of sections of the population that had hitherto been shut out from the benefits of post-school education, and that has been a great democratic good which present financial or other difficulties should not lead us to discount. But this does not mean that all these students are, or should be, studying the traditional, intensively taught, undergraduate degrees in the liberal arts and sciences as full-time, immediately post-18 students at residential universities. There is a wholly legitimate place in a diversified higher education system for all kinds of part-time, work-related, vocationally oriented, career-break, courses, but the social value of the institutions that primarily provide such courses should be recognized and properly rewarded without forcing them to try to ape 'traditional' universities when the odds, in terms of resources, reputation, and so on, are so stacked against them.

To understand the real significance of Browne's proposals, we need briefly to recall the evolution of the present system over the past half century. In the 1960s and 1970s, the bulk of British universities' income came to them in the form of a 'block grant' from government, administered to them on the 'arm's length' principle by a body, largely made up of senior academics, called the University Grants Committee. In the 1980s, this system underwent substantial modification, with, for example, the 'research' element being distributed differentially in accordance with the results of successive Research Assessment Exercises, while the element covering teaching was paid on roughly a per capita basis, with higher multiples for expensive subjects such as medicine. In the late 1980s, the UGC was replaced by what has become the Higher Education Funding Council, whose membership includes business people and administrators and whose role has been to give effect to successive government policies more directly by tying funding to the implementation of so-called reforms. In the course of the 1980s and 1990s, Conservative governments deliberately reduced the level of funding while increasing student numbers: in the years between 1989 and 1997 alone, as the Browne Report itself acknowledges, 'universities experienced a drop in funding per student of 36%'. The decision in 1992 to allow all polytechnics to become universities almost doubled the number of universities, and therefore of university students, overnight, all now to be funded under the single system. Between 1981 and 1997 considerable damage was done to universities, not least to the quality of their teaching, by this deliberate combination of headlong expansion and progressive lowering of funding levels.

In the mid-1990s a committee was established, chaired by Lord Dearing, an experienced education policy-fixer, to come up with ways of halting this downward spiral. Its 1997 report was taken to signal the end of 'universal free higher education tuition', since it recommended that graduates should make a direct financial contribution to the costs of their courses. Dearing suggested that this should be done through a system of deferred repayments of an initial loan, calibrated according to income after university. But David Blunkett, the relevant minister at the time, decided it should be imposed as an upfront charge, initially of £1,000 per year (he also, in an equally ill-considered move, reduced maintenance grants). Most students felt worse off; most universities felt very little better off. It was clear from the outset that 'Blunkett's botch' could only be, at best, a temporary repair.

The Higher Education Act 2004, the occasion of bitter political conflict and the narrowest of victories in Parliament by the government, replaced this fudge with a system of variable fees whose level was to be set by individual universities, up to a maximum of £3,000, indexed to inflation. The Act also scrapped upfront payment, and instituted the present system of deferred repayment (not starting till the graduate's income exceeds £15,000), together with a confusing mixture of bursaries, grants, and other loans. The stated aim of allowing universities to set their own fees was to encourage institutions to 'compete on price'. As it turned out, only one institution charged below the maximum: it thereby missed out on quite a bit of money, and soon all universities charged the same maximum fee. This has brought universities some welcome extra income and allowed them to begin to address some of the problems caused by long-term underfunding, but it is still the case that the costs of teaching are principally met from the block grant.

When considering Browne's proposals, it is important to realize four things about the present system. First, the existence of the block grant allows universities both a degree of flexibility about its use (as, for example, in cross-subsidizing less popular subjects) and a degree of stability in their forward planning (at least between successive funding settlements). Second, it is still up to individual universities to make educational decisions about the range of subjects they offer, the best forms of teaching them, and so on; the government does not prescribe these, and applicants simply choose from among those the universities provide. Third, the government has a direct financial interest in regulating total student numbers since its expenditure is per capita, both in terms of the block grant and the underwriting of the costs of the loan and bursary systems. And fourth, fees are not determined by the actual cost of the student's education, since these vary between courses and between universities; the current fee is better understood as a kind of graduate poll tax, softened by a mildly progressive deferred payment arrangement. What we have at present, therefore, represents an intricate kind of compact between the state, the universities, the students, and the taxpayer.

Browne proposes to scrap most of this. In its place, he wants to see a system in which the universities are providers of services, students are the (rational) consumers of those services, and the state plays the role of the regulator. His premise is that 'Students are best placed to make the judgement about what they want to get from participating in higher education.' His frequently repeated mantra is, 'Student choice will drive up quality,' and the measure of quality is 'student satisfaction'. At the moment, he laments, 'students do not have the opportunity to choose between institutions on the basis of price and value for money.' Under his scheme, such value will be primarily judged by students in terms of 'the employment returns from their courses'. Courses that lead to higher earnings will be able to charge higher fees. The same assumption governs repayment rates: 'Graduates will be required to make a higher contribution to the costs of higher education varying widely according to how much benefit they have received from studying,' where the amount of benefit is indicated by the size of their subsequent salary. Overall, 'increasing competition for students will mean that institutions will have stronger incentives to focus on improving teaching quality. If they are not able to attract enough students, their funding will decrease,' and they will eventually be eliminated. Perfect competition theory rules, OK?

Naturally, the report presents all this as being for the greater good of universities: 'We have made the case that investment in higher education should increase; the decision on whether this case is convincing will rest with students.' This is culpably misleading. The report proposes a huge, almost unimaginable, de facto cut in investment in higher education. It then says that it hopes to see this enormous shortfall made good by the fees students will be willing to pay to those institutions that convince them they are worth it (principally by enabling them to earn a higher salary). It is in reality a disguised voucher scheme. Students will be able to borrow the cost of the fees, on somewhat subsidized terms, and they are then expected to go and spend them on the 'service provider' of their choice. The report proposes that what universities teach will henceforth be determined by their anticipation of consumer demand.

And even in its own most wildly optimistic terms, this report proposes a hefty cut in funding. In suggesting that the standard fee should initially be set at £6,000 (which particular institutions might choose to exceed, though there will be various disincentives, including a 'levy' which would claw some of it back), Browne acknowledges that this would not fully replace the value of the block grant even for the most successful institutions. But this is shrugged off with that kind of *je m'en foutisme* about real consequences that it is so much easier to cultivate in the boardroom than on the shopfloor: 'The purpose of starting the levy at a lower point is to instil a focus on efficiency throughout the system.' Lots of courses may have to be closed and lots of people sacked, but that must mean, by definition, that they weren't offering a product the consumer wanted, so good riddance.

Much discussion has been focused on the fact that the stronger universities would be likely to charge fees well above the standard level, and that this would introduce a 'two-tier' (or, in reality, a multi-tier) system. But the fact is that we have a multi-tier system already, with both the better-qualified applicants and the bulk of research funding being attracted to the universities that (are thought to) have the best reputations. The most likely effect of Browne's proposals here would be to exacerbate the financial disparity between types of university and, above all, to bring about a much closer correlation between the reputational hierarchy of institutions and the social class of their student body. The report includes various 'access' regulations intended to mitigate the more extreme effects of this re-allocation of students by family wealth, but differential fees are, of course, absolutely central to its conception of how the market mechanism will operate, and it is a necessary truth about markets that they tend to replicate and even intensify the existing distribution of economic power. 'Free competition' between rich and poor consumers means Harrods for the former and Aldi for the latter: that's what the punters have 'chosen'.

The character, but perhaps also the confusions, of this model come more clearly into focus if we return to the statement I quoted earlier which says: 'Students are best placed to make the judgement about what they want to get from participating in higher education.' Looked at more closely, this statement reveals itself to be a vacuous tautology because of its reliance on the phrase 'want to get'. By definition, individuals are privileged reporters on what they think they *want*. The sentence could only do the work the report requires of it if it said something more like: 'Students are best placed to make the judgement about what they should get from participating in higher education.' But this proposition is obviously false. Children may be best placed to judge what they *want* to get from the sweetshop, but they are not best placed to judge what they *should* get from their schooling. University students are, of course, no longer children, but nor are they simply rational consumers in a perfect market.

It is fascinating, and very revealing, to see how Browne's unreal confidence in the rationality of subjective consumer choice is matched by his lack of belief in reasoned argument and judgement. The sentence that immediately follows the vacuous one about students 'wants' reads: 'We have looked carefully at the scope to distribute funding by some objective metric of quality; but there is no robust way to do this and we doubt whether the choices of a central funding body should be put before those of students.' It is, first of all, striking that the only alternative envisaged to the random play of subjective consumer choice is an 'objective metric of quality', i.e. some quantitative indicator. And secondly, it is no less striking that instead of allowing that an informed judgement might be based on reasons, arguments, and evidence, there are simply the 'choices' made by two groups, treated as though they are just two equivalent expressions of subjective preference. We can have the money for a national system of higher education distributed either in accordance with the tastes of 18-year-olds or in accordance with the tastes of a group of older people in London; there's no other way to do it.

Similarly, Browne appears to believe that the only relevant measure of teaching quality is 'student satisfaction'. That is how the system will work: if they are satisfied, they'll pay, and if not, not; and the pressure they exert thereby will 'drive up quality'. But this, other problems aside, comes perilously close to reducing important human experiences to a set of 'preferences' as reported on a tick-box questionnaire. I would hope the students I teach come away with certain kinds of dissatisfaction (including with themselves: a 'satisfied' student is nigh-on ineducable), and it matters more that they carry on wondering about the source of that dissatisfaction than whether they 'liked' the course or not. This is another respect in which the 'consumer' model is simply misleading, an error encouraged by the prevalence in current edspeak of the category of 'the student experience' (many universities now have a senior figure entitled 'Pro-Vice-Chancellor, Student Experience'). It may be that the most appropriate way to decide whether the atmosphere in the student bar is right is by whether students say, when asked in a questionnaire, that they 'like' it or not. But this is obviously not the best way to decide whether a philosophy degree should have a compulsory course in Kant. The philosophy department might hope that, some time after graduation, most of its former students would come to see the wisdom of this requirement, but 'student satisfaction' is not what is at issue here. And the retrospective character of this recognition tells us something important about education: individuals often need to be told by someone who knows that a particular line of study is *worth* pursuing whether at the time they *want* to or not.

The Browne report, in keeping with the ethos of market populism, shies away from anything that might look to involve a judgement that one activity is more worthwhile than another: all you can go by are consumer preferences, what people say they think they want. But at certain moments the report is forced to fall back on other criteria which then reveal the hollowness of the central premise. For example, when the report is suggesting that there would be some residual functions for a re-jigged Higher Education Council, it allows that there might be a 'public interest' in making sure there were enough courses in, say, medicine, and then goes on: 'The costs of these courses are high and, if students were asked to meet all of these costs, there is a risk that they would choose to study cheaper courses instead.' Or again, when proposing a limited amount of 'targeted investment by the public in certain courses' (essentially in science and technology), it concedes that this would be necessary since 'students may not choose these courses because the private returns are not as high as other courses, the costs are higher and there are cheaper courses on offer, or simply because these courses are perceived as more difficult.' Wait just a minute! Browne's guiding assumption – the nag on which the nation's higher education inheritance is to be gambled – is that the system will be governed by student choice. If they can see that it is worth their while to study, say, medicine, even if its costs are higher, they will choose to do so and courses in medicine will therefore be provided; and if the students think these courses do not represent 'value for money', then they will shun them, in which case either the cost of such courses will fall or they will simply die out. But now Browne is admitting market failure: applicants might make 'irrational' decisions. And what's more, where are these judgements about what is 'needed' coming from? We've just been told that the 'choices' of central bodies should give way before the 'choices' of students, but now that only seems to be true in some cases.

It is, incidentally, one of the several dispiriting features of this report that even when it shows an inconsistent twitch of non-market reflexes and recognizes that there may be a public interest in making sure that certain subjects are offered and studied, it in effect confines these subjects to science and technology (with a token nod to the possible economic usefulness of some foreign languages). The only social value the report seems able to think of is economic: these subjects contribute directly to the economy, it is alleged, and so we must have them. By implication, the others, especially the arts and humanities, are just optional extras. If students are willing to cash in their voucher to study them – perhaps because, for some unexamined reason, they are thought to lead to higher-paying jobs – so be it; but if they're not, then there's no public interest in having them. Despite the occasional (very occasional) mention of, say, 'culture', the logic of the report's proposals gives such values no independent standing. Overwhelmingly, the general statements announce, with startling confidence, what the real point of higher education is: 'Higher education matters because it drives innovation and economic transformation. Higher education helps to produce economic growth, which in turn contributes to national prosperity.' And just when you might think there was going to be a glimpse of something broader, your knuckles are smartly rapped: 'Higher education matters because it transforms the lives of individuals. On graduating, graduates are more likely to be employed, more likely to enjoy higher wages and better job satisfaction, and more likely to find it easier to move from one job to the next.' This report displays no real interest in universities as places of education; they are conceived of simply as engines of economic prosperity and as agencies for equipping future employees to earn higher salaries.

But although this is what higher education is said to be for, Browne complains that it does not at present fulfil its function very well; it does not 'meet business needs'. For example; 'The CBI found that 48% of employers were dissatisfied with the business awareness of the graduates they hired.' Oh dear! Can it be that some universities may not have a compulsory 'business awareness day' each week? But don't worry, Browne's proposals will fix that. Only courses that lead to high-paying jobs will survive, so universities will make sure they provide the graduates that high-paying employers want. And anyway, many students will have developed more 'business awareness' through the very experience of seeing how failing businesses are driven to respond to falling market share.

The truth is, of course, that universities are not businesses and they do not operate in a market (which is not to say that they do not need to be financially well run and to make good use of their, at present largely public, resources). All comparisons and analogies are potentially misleading, but it would be less inaccurate to say that historically British universities have been national cultural institutions that more closely resembled, say, the British Museum or the BBC rather than, say, British Home Stores or BP. This does, of course, leave them vulnerable to the winds of political fashion, not just in terms of fluctuations in funding but also in such matters as the recent mania for constant assessment. As a result, some people see the idea of the better-regarded and better-off British universities 'going private' as appealing, a form of liberation from the heavy hand of the state, and some, overtly or secretly, hope that the adoption of Browne's proposals will hasten this outcome. But while it may be true that the present system embodies an unnecessary pretence that all institutions called universities perform the same set of functions, it is no good deluding ourselves that simply leaving 18-year-old applicants to cash their vouchers at a university of their choice will lead to a more intelligently conceived provision of diverse, high-quality institutions. It may just lead to a few private jets and a lot of Ryanairs.

II

The scale of the report's dismantling of the public character of higher education is breathtaking, and yet, from another point of view, it is scarcely surprising. Though described as 'an independent review', it was never likely to issue in a set of recommendations so out of tune with current government thinking that they would simply be ignored. The coalition is at the moment using the whipped-up frenzy about the deficit in the public finances as a cover for a recognizably ideological assault on all forms of public provision. There was, presumably, little chance that this report would make proposals that were not congruent with the form that is to be given to this assault by the Current Spending Review. So Browne has wielded the axe in advance, not trimming public expenditure on teaching in universities but more or less completely abolishing it. There will remain some minor residual functions to be performed by a new Higher Education Council, for which £700 million seems to be allocated, and there will of course be the initial costs of subsidizing the proposed loan scheme. But the dramatic centrepiece of the report sees almost the entire block grant for teaching (some £3.2bn) being returned to the Exchequer. Some representatives of British universities, so appalled and terrified by the consequences of the massive cuts likely to be proposed in the Current Spending Review, appear to be pinning their hopes on Browne as the only way of getting any money into higher education. These are certainly desperate times, but perhaps the case for the proper public funding of universities should not be surrendered quite so readily. What has to be recognized is that the Browne report is not some alternative, still less antidote, to the Spending Review: they go together as the two faces of a calculated attempt to re-shape higher education in this country by subjecting it to 'the discipline of the market'.

Browne presents his proposals as a package, with a single sustaining logic, and it is noticeable that in interview he has been insistent that no one should try to unpick the package. But Vince Cable, David Willetts, and their colleagues may be well advised to adopt his proposals on a strictly selective basis. Fees will clearly rise, in which case features of the report's scheme for repayment are preferable to the present system: better-paid graduates would pay proportionately more, lower-paid graduates proportionately less. For maintenance costs, its combination of a uniform loan and a more generous means-tested grant would also benefit the students who need it most. In addition, the report is clearly right that part-time students must be eligible for funding for their tuition on the same basis, pro rata, as full-time students; the lack of such provision was a major flaw of the 2004 legislation. In these respects, several of the details of Browne's scheme are quite progressive.

But these are, precisely, details. It is difficult to estimate – though some reports suggest it may be difficult to exaggerate – the damage that may be done to British universities in the short term by the abolition of the block grant and the wild hope that its functions will be taken over by some kind of market mechanism run by university applicants. At present, the block grant is the tangible expression of the public interest in the provision of good-quality education across the system, and the means for universities to make informed intellectual choices about the subjects they teach. But before Liberal Democrat MPs sell their souls in the division lobbies, they need to consider the longer-term consequences for British education and culture more generally of implementing the kind of reasoning on which this report is based. What is at stake here is not primarily the question of whether this or that group of graduates will pay a little more or a little less towards the costs of their education, even though that may seem (particularly to those in marginal seats) to be the most potent element electorally. What is at stake is whether universities in the future are to be thought of as having a public cultural role partly sustained by public support, or whether we move further towards re-defining them in terms of a purely economistic calculation of value and a wholly individualist conception of 'consumer satisfaction'.

18 October 2010

The Browne report proposed removing all direct public funding for teaching in the arts and humanities, confining the residual element of public support to the scientific and technological subjects. In adopting the essence of this proposal, the coalition government emphasized that the same level of funding was being withdrawn from all subjects, but that the greater expense involved in teaching the scientific and technological subjects meant that they needed to be partly supported directly by public funds rather than entirely by the new student fees, as would now be true for the arts and humanities. This followed the decision taken by the previous government to ring-fence the funding of research in the sciences at the expense of reductions for the humanities. In order to bring out the peculiar nature of the logic of these decisions and to remind representatives of all disciplines of their common cause, I published a short tongue-in-cheek parody which imagined how the case would look if these priorities were reversed.

A central feature of the government's higher education proposals is the complete withdrawal of funding for the teaching of science and technology subjects. The proposals recognize that arts, humanities, and social science subjects are essential to society's well-being, and therefore the small residual amount left in the teaching budget will be devoted to supporting these disciplines.

This policy is said to be consistent with the government's emphasis on economic growth. An educated, flexible, and creative workforce is vital to every sector of the economy, and the contribution of an education in the humanities to fostering just these qualities is well understood. The bulk of those who have risen to the top of large corporations were educated in these subjects, and their recruitment policies continue to confirm the value of such graduates to their organizations.

Insofar as the government acknowledges any other goals, it places a strong emphasis on questions of civic commitment, cultural literacy, national identity, and democratic citizenship, and so naturally it wishes to devote the bulk of available resources to supporting the humanities. The study of subjects such as history, philosophy, literature, and politics enables citizens better to place current issues in a wider framework, to address the hidden assumptions behind plausible claims, to be alert to the power of language, and to appreciate the complexity of Britain's place in the wider world.

And finally, it is hardly surprising that the government would decide to concentrate funding on the humanities, since the overwhelming majority of ministers themselves studied these disciplines at university, and so they are well aware of how such training in clear thinking, close analysis, and lucid expression have helped to develop their own capacities and been the foundation for their successful careers. This probably also explains their frequent gibes about 'mickey-mouse' courses in some science subjects and their mockery of (US inspired) PhD topics in these fields as over-specialized, over-theorized, and over here.

This one-sided emphasis on the importance and utility of the humanities sets a difficult challenge to the champions of the scientific and technological subjects, always the cinderellas of British higher education. Proponents of the sciences tend to respond by arguing that a 'two cultures' model is misleading and out of date. They argue that all disciplines cultivate our intellectual and imaginative powers, and moreover that it is impossible for many of the insights and analyses derived from the humanities to be given proper effect in the world unless we understand the laws of nature, the properties of matter, and so on.

In more aggressive mode, some of them point out that the decision, following the Browne review, to provide funding exclusively for humanities subjects betrays a lack of confidence in the power of those subjects to attract the best young minds. If the humanities are said to be both so intrinsically compelling and socially useful, then surely sufficient applicants will choose to study them anyway? And if the government really believes in student choice, as it professes to do, then it should be happy to see students flocking to the sciences instead, even if some of these courses (in, say, astronomy or theoretical physics) don't look like direct preparation for employment. It does have to be acknowledged that in recent years several universities have had to close their chemistry or physics departments, citing lack of student demand, but the champions of science argue that, as with the similar predicament of some departments of modern languages, this is more the result of the faulty structure of the national curriculum than any indication of the dispensability of these subjects.

The more reflective spokespersons for the sciences recognize that it is self-defeating to try to rest their case exclusively on arguments about their disciplines' contribution to material prosperity. It is not just that the direct contribution to economic growth of subjects such as neuroscience or pure mathematics would be difficult to demonstrate, especially when compared to more immediately practical subjects such as moral philosophy or media studies. It is, rather, that the very character and purpose of the sciences takes us so far beyond questions of prosperity. The drive for fuller understanding of our physical world is in principle limitless in much the same way that the search for fuller understanding of our human world is. It cannot be arbitrarily constrained or directed in the interests of some immediate economic gain. The sciences are, ultimately, expressive of the mind's search for order and of our need to situate ourselves in the universe.

It is hard to believe that highly educated ministers can be unaware of these truths, yet they persist in their baffling decision to favour some disciplines at the expense of others. Perhaps representatives of the sciences need to mount a wider campaign for public support. Being sucked in to the government's own restrictive agenda about increasing the GDP may not be the way to go. Instead, they should surely tap into the great well-spring of public interest in and curiosity about scientific enquiry, as evidenced by the eager audiences for public lectures, panel discussions, radio talks, TV programmes and so on (the level of interest shown in such settings is almost as great as that shown when the subject-matter is something to do with literature, history or philosophy). Although some science subjects may be thought less intellectually demanding than, say, literary criticism or art history, it should still be recognized that many bright sixth-formers choose to study them, and the case for the support of these subjects at university level goes beyond the present generation. After all, parents of the future will not want their children to be confined to the study just of the humanities or directly vocational subjects.

In their turn, representatives of the humanities should not take a selfish or complacent view just because their budgets have been ring-fenced in the past and look to be favoured in the future. They, too, should recognize that a broad base of support needs to be built up to sustain education and research across a wide front. No one would want to see the British Academy or the Arts and Humanities Research Council treating the Royal Society or the science research councils as poor relations, still less as competitors to be outmanoeuvred in the scramble for funds. Public investment in education in the sciences is one hallmark of a civilized society. Can it really be that, in addition to the other ways in which current proposals will damage the future of higher education in this country, a short-sighted attempt is going to be made to favour the humanities at the direct expense of the sciences? If so, surely protest is called for. Nerds of the world unite – you have nothing to lose but your anoraks.

30 November 2010

Epilogue: A Complex Inheritance

This book has not tried to provide a comprehensive analysis of the nature and functions of higher education, nor has it tried to come up with new proposals for its funding. It has, instead, engaged critically with a range of assumptions about, and policies towards, universities, and in so doing it has attempted to suggest some better starting-points for discussion and a more appropriate set of idioms in which to conduct that discussion. It has principally concentrated on the idea that universities provide a home for attempts to extend and deepen human understanding in ways which are, simultaneously, disciplined and illimitable. This enterprise can have any number of beneficial side-effects – even helping students to develop and refine their own capacities for understanding can to some extent be seen as a side-effect as well as a central function – and public debate tends to concentrate on those incidental or contingent outcomes. For that reason, this book has subjected those benefits to somewhat quizzical analysis, suggesting that we may have allowed the felt need for justification to distort or over-ride the prior task of characterization. And, finally, the book, especially in Part Two, has deliberately revisited certain moments in recent decades when a particular proposal or policy was first under discussion in order to highlight the continuity of the underlying assumptions and their damaging consequences, and thus to emphasize the continuing need for criticism that challenges these assumptions. Critique, it is worth saying again, need not be 'merely negative'; it can be a medium for allowing more adequate principles to infiltrate public debate in ways that most readers may find more engaging and ultimately more persuasive than a case made in heavily abstract and systematic terms.

However, although there are underlying continuities among the proposals discussed in Part Two, those chapters also bear witness to what has been a rapidly accelerating process of change as the deliberate assault on the autonomy of universities has intensified. For example, the degree to which large elements of research funding are now confined to so-called 'national priorities' – topics which the government itself, not the researchers in the relevant fields, deems it 'worth' researching – constitutes a level of direct interference that simply would not have been countenanced twenty years ago. Similarly, the imposition of commercial priorities and the requirement that universities serve the needs of business has reflected the growing confidence of those who speak for 'the economy' that they have an unchallengeable legitimacy which they believe those who represent culture, intellect, and education simply cannot match. Seen in this context, 'impact' is not, as some of its academic defenders would have it, a modest and sensible attempt to demonstrate the wider 'social value' of research: it represents another instalment in the attempt to prioritize non-intellectual over intellectual criteria in evaluating scholarly and scientific enquiry, with the deliberate intention of redirecting future research towards activities that yield measurable economic and social outcomes.

Although this general direction of change reflects deeper social forces than the temporary possession of power by one or other of the major parties, it is also important to be aware of the ways policy fluctuates in response to more immediate political and electoral circumstances. There have been important shifts even since I completed the first draft of this book. Britain has had a new Conservative-dominated coalition government since May 2010, and it has lost no time in making its mark on universities. It has adopted the central proposals of the Browne Review, discussed in Chapter 10, revolutionizing the basis on which Britain's universities are financed, though full details of how the new system will operate have yet to be announced. From 2012, the direct public funding of teaching costs will be replaced by indirect private funding in the form of income from student fees (supplemented by a continuing but reduced subsidy in the case of the more expensive scientific and technological subjects). The government will make loans available to cover these fees and will then recover the costs through a graduate contribution levied once income exceeds a given threshold. At this point, no one – not the government, not the universities, and certainly not the public – can know what the consequences of these changes will be. A great many untested assumptions are involved – about how potential university applicants will respond to the prospect of increased debt, about how undergraduates will behave if they are increasingly treated as consumers, about how universities will decide what to 'charge' and what to teach, and about much else besides. It seems certain that Britain's universities will become even more markedly stratified, with those at the upper end of the reputational hierarchy commanding ever more of the income from research and fees and thus probably maintaining a broad spread of subject-offerings, while those less favoured may concentrate on high-volume vocational courses. It also seems likely that, apart from a targeted number of beneficiaries of bursary schemes, recruitment to the traditional arts and sciences courses at the more favoured universities will increasingly be from among the children of the comfortably off middle and upper-middle classes. How the arts and humanities will fare under this regime, and what kinds of 'new providers' may enter the 'market' selling cheaper and perhaps shorter degree courses, are among the other unknowns. The one thing that can be said is that direct public funding, having once been removed, is unlikely ever to be restored at its previous level.

But I should like to end by reiterating that a discussion of what is of interest and importance about universities should not be confined to the topical question of how they are to be funded. As I have repeatedly emphasized, this question practically monopolizes public discussion at present, and there is a danger, first, of sliding almost unconsciously into the habit of re-describing intellectual activity entirely in terms of what might be thought to 'justify public funding', and then, secondly, of becoming unable to throw off a defensive posture, an air of expecting a hostile or unsympathetic reaction to this case. One of the most dispiriting features of the current climate of discussion is the background implication, discernible in the comments of some journalists and politicians, that universities are something of a luxury whose rationale is not likely to survive properly searching scrutiny and that many academics are little better than middle-class welfare-scroungers, indulging their hobbies at public expense. This has been evident in, to take just one example, some of the commentary on the continuing debate over the 'impact' proposals, where it seems simply taken for granted that anyone objecting to these (badly formulated and ill thought-out) proposals must be expressing a complacent sense of entitlement to public funding of their activities whether they are of any value or not. Engagement on these terms is almost bound to be fruitless and is a waste of spirit. We need to start from somewhere else, and this book has tried to provide a few pointers to what a better starting-point might look like.

One helpful opening move, as I've tried to suggest throughout, may be to consider what it is that we value and admire about good work in scholarship and science, and then to reflect on the conditions which seem conducive to its achievement. Universities are not quite the only places where such work is done, even now, but they unquestionably represent much the biggest concentration of such enquiry. It may be that the public perception of universities focuses too narrowly on their teaching role (undergraduate teaching above all), seeing them perhaps as bigger and more sophisticated sixth-form colleges. This role is certainly central to most universities, but it is far from being the whole story. Major universities are complex organisms, fostering an extraordinary variety of intellectual, scientific and cultural activity, and the significance and value of much that goes on within them cannot be restricted to a single national framework or to the present generation. They have become an important medium – perhaps the single most important institutional medium – for conserving, understanding, extending, and handing on to subsequent generations the intellectual, scientific, and artistic heritage of mankind. In thinking about the conditions necessary for their flourishing, we should not, therefore, take too short-term or too purely local a view.

Adopting this wider perspective may also help us become more aware of the limitations of treating economic growth as the overriding test of value. Taking a longer-term view of the history, and indeed the future, of universities encourages us to ask fundamental questions of the goal of 'contributing to national economic prosperity'. For example, how much prosperity do we need (and who counts as 'we')? Is it desirable at any cost? What is it, in its turn, good for? And so on. Any serious attempt to address these questions will inevitably have to invoke non-economic values. Most people recognize the standing of such values in their own lives – they do not care for their partners or their children in order to generate a profit any more than they admire a beautiful view or a natural wonder because it increases employment – but, as I have suggested, it has become difficult to appeal to such values in a public sphere whose discourse is chiefly framed by the combination of individualism and instrumentalism. Universities are not just good places in which to undertake such fundamental questioning; they also embody an alternative set of values in their very rationale. Attending to these values may help us remember, amid difficult and distracting circumstances, that we are merely custodians for the present generation of a complex intellectual inheritance which we did not create – and which is not ours to destroy.

References

Introduction

p. x 'living "wisely, agreeably, and well"'. John Maynard Keynes, *Essays in Persuasion* (London, Macmillan, 1931), p. 328.

PART ONE
1. The Global Multiversity?

p. 6 'now carried on in a major research university'. Clark Kerr, *The Uses of the University* (Cambridge, Mass.: Harvard University Press, 5th edn 2001 [1st pub. 1963]).

p. 11 'to give the past its place in us'. David Wootton, 'Formal Feelings for History' [review of Neil MacGregor, *A History of the World in 100 Objects*], *Times Literary Supplement*, 24 September 2010, p. 17.

p. 15 'Global knowledge-sharing and communications'. John Aubrey Douglass, C. Judson King, and Irwin Feller (eds.), *Globalization's Muse: Universities and Higher Education Systems in a Changing World* (Berkeley, Calif: Berkeley Public Policy Press, 2009), pp. 5–7.

2. Universities in Britain: A Very Short History

p. 21 'developments can be measured and found wanting.' See, for example, Duke Maskell and Ian Robinson, *The New Idea of a University* (London: Haven Books, 2001).

p. 21 'acutely different cultural meanings and purposes'. Sheldon Rothblatt, *Tradition and Change in English Liberal Education: An Essay in History and Culture* (London: Faber, 1976), p. 205.

p. 22 'over the course of the last millennium'. Walter Rüegg (ed.), *A History of the University in Europe*, Vol. III: *Universities in the Nineteenth and Early Twentieth Centuries (1800–1945)* (Cambridge: Cambridge University Press, 2004), p. ii.

p. 36 '(including Berkeley and UCLA)'. Cristina Gonzalez, *Clark Kerr's University of California: Leadership, Diversity, and Planning in Higher Education* (New Brunswick, NJ: Transaction, 2011).

3. The Useful and the Useless

p. 40 'the country's economic performance in the twenty-first century'. Department of Business, Innovation, and Skills, *Higher Ambitions: The Future of Universities in a Knowledge Economy* (London: HMSO, 2009), p. 9.

p. 40 'public ideals of higher education'. John Henry Newman, *The Idea of a University*, ed. Frank M. Turner (New Haven: Yale University Press, 1996), p. 282 (unless otherwise indicated, all quotations from Newman are taken from this edition without individual page numbers being given).

p. 40 'the idea of the university ever written in any language'. Jaroslav Pelikan, *The Idea of a University: A Re-examination* (New Haven: Yale University Press, 1992), p. 9.

p. 41 'a common grievance over parking'. Kerr, *The Uses of the University*, p. 15.

p. 43 'composite volume with a complex bibliographic history'. A full bibliographic history is given in Ian Ker's annotated edition of *The Idea of a University* (Oxford: Clarendon Press, 1976).

p. 46 ' so happily as the office of a Professor'. Newman's reflection in 1833, when he was considering standing for the Chair of Moral Philosophy at Oxford; quoted in Ian Ker, *John Henry Newman: A Biography* (Oxford: Oxford University Press, 2009 [1st pub. 1988]), p. 90.

p. 49 'articles in the *Edinburgh Review* between 1808 and 1810'. See Asa Briggs, 'Oxford and its Critics, 1800–1835', in M. G. Brock and M. C. Curthoys (eds.), *The History of the University of Oxford*, Vol. VI: *Nineteenth-Century Oxford* (Oxford: Oxford University Press, 1997), part 1, pp. 134–45.

p. 58 'At Liverpool and Birmingham.' Quoted in Rothblatt, *Tradition and Change in English Liberal Education*, p. 186.

p. 59 'a framed photograph of Newman'. H. S. Jones, *Intellect and Character in Victorian England: Mark Pattison and the Invention of the Don* (Cambridge: Cambridge University Press, 2007), p. 9.

4. The Character of the Humanities

p. 63 'was by then uncontroversial'. J. H. Plumb (ed.), *Crisis in the Humanities* (Harmondsworth: Penguin, 1964).

p. 65 'justifications of "great books" courses'. For a useful recent account of these discussions, see Louis Menand, *The Marketplace of Ideas: Reform and Resistance in the American University* (New York: Norton, 2010).

p. 66 'never lose their pertinence'. E. P. Thompson, *The Making of the English Working Class* (London: Gollancz, 1963); Frank Kermode, *The Sense of an Ending: Studies in the Theory of Fiction* (New York: Oxford University Press, 1967); John Rawls, *A Theory of Justice* (New York: Oxford University Press, 1971).

p. 67 'so much else has changed'. A. C. Bradley, *Shakespearian Tragedy* (London: Macmillan, 1904).

p. 80 'have to look up the "results"'. Thomas Mann, 'Nietzsche's Philosophy in the Light of Recent History' (1947), in *Last Essays*, trans. Richard and Clara Winston and Tania and James Stern (New York; Knopf, 1959).

p. 85 'and are created by it'. Sir Adam Roberts, introduction to *Past, Present and Future: The Public Value of Humanities and Social Sciences* (London: British Academy, 2010).

5. The Highest Aspirations and Ideals

p. 86 'the community's highest aspirations and ideals'. Thorstein Veblen, *The Higher Learning in America: A Memorandum on the Conduct of Universities by Businessmen* (New York: Huebsch, 1918), p. 34.

p. 94 'fail again, fail better'. Samuel Beckett, *Worstward Ho* (London: Calder, 1983), p. 47.

p. 98 'and must be willing to bear the expense of it'. John Adams, from a letter of 1785, quoted in Andrew Delbanco, 'The Universities in Trouble', *New York Review of Books*, 14 May 2009.

p. 98 '"great books" course at college'. Martha Nussbaum, *Not for Profit: Why Democracy Needs the Humanities* (Princeton: Princeton University Press, 2010).

p. 100 'the economic and social benefits of the disciplines they represent'. *Leading the World: The Economic Impact of UK Arts and Humanities Research* (London: AHRC, 2009); and *Past, Present and Future: The Public Value of Humanities and Social Sciences* (London: British Academy, 2010).

p. 109 '"no standing still" conception of excellence'. Gordon Graham, *Universities: The Recovery of an Idea* (Exeter: Imprint Academic, 2002), p. 59.

p. 109 'the vacuity of "excellence" as it is used in these contexts'. Bill Readings, *The University in Ruins* (Cambridge, Mass.: Harvard University Press, 1996).

p. 111 'capable of shutting off the sun and the stars because they do not pay a dividend'. John Maynard Keynes, 'National Self-Sufficiency', *New Statesman and Nation*, 8/15 July 1933.

PART TWO

Prologue

p. 118 'and like that it produces its effect by *repetition*'. John Stuart Mill (1833), in *The Collected Works of John Stuart Mill*, ed. J. M. Robson, 33 vols (Toronto: University of Toronto Press, 1963–91), vol.1, p.372.

p. 118 'qualitatively different and dependent on new circumstances in the society'. W. B. Carnochan, *The Battleground of the Curriculum: Liberal Education and American Experience* (Stanford: Stanford University Press, 1993), pp. 5–6.

6. Bibliometry

p. 131 'to address the problem more realistically'. Robert Jackson, Chevening discussion paper on '"Manpower Planning" in Higher Education', in Stuart Maclure, 'A Nudge Towards the Market-Place', *Policy Studies*, 9 (1989), 11–18.

p. 131 'the process of national renovation which is now underway'. See Michael Boon, 'His Kampf: The Muddle at the UFC', *Public Money and Management*, 11 (1991), 33–4.

7. The Business Analogy

p. 134 'Analogies never walk on all fours'. For the complex history of this phrase, see S. T. Coleridge, *Aids to Reflection* [1825], ed. John Beer (Princeton: Princeton University Press, 1993), p.141, 11. 21.

p. 146 'to philosophize is to learn to die'. Michel de Montaigne, *The Complete Essays*, ed. M. A. Screech (Harmondsworth: Penguin, 1993), Essay XX.

8. HiEdBizUK

p. 161 'one of the great state papers of this century'. John Carswell, *Government and the Universities in Britain: Programme and Performance 1960–1980* (Cambridge: Cambridge University Press, 1985), p. 38.

p. 161 'and we consider its effects to be harmful'. *Higher Education: Report of the Committee Appointed by the Prime Minister under the Chairmanship of Lord Robbins 1961–63*, Cmnd. 2154 (London: HMSO, 1963), p. 178.

10. Browne's Gamble

p. 190 'conception of "consumer satisfaction"'. When first published in the *London Review of Books*, this chapter provoked a response (admirably civil and carefully argued, if unpersuasive) from David Willetts, the Minister for Universities and Science: 'The Arts, Humanities and Social Sciences in the Modern University', http://nds.coi.gov.uk/content/ (accessed 5 March 2011).

Epilogue

p. 197 'at its previous level'. The Goverment's White Paper *Higher Education: Student at the Heart of the system* was published at tie end of June 2011, after this book had been completed. For an extended critical analysis of its assumptions and its reasoning, see my 'From Robbins to McKinsey, *London Review of Books*, 33: 16 (25 August 2011), pp. 9–14.

Acknowledgements

Universities are highly collaborative places, and in writing this book, more perhaps than any other, I have been given much support and encouragement by friends and colleagues, including colleagues (in the larger sense) from elsewhere in Britain and elsewhere in the world. It would be impracticable to include here a consolidated list of names, but I hope this book's dedication signals my sense of indebtedness to this wider world of discussion and scholarship. For practical help of various kinds, I am grateful to my agent, Peter Robinson of Rogers, Coleridge and White, and to my editor, Alexis Kirschbaum at Penguin Books. My greatest debts are to those friends who read, criticized, and improved this book in its successive typescript versions: Peter Clarke, Angela Leighton, Ruth Morse, Jeremy Mynott, Helen Small, John Thompson, and Donald Winch.

The greater part of this book has not previously been published in any form. This is true of the Introduction, Chapters 1 to 5, the Prologue to Part Two, and the Epilogue, except that some paragraphs in Chapter 2 have been reworked from an essay in the *London Review of Books* published in 2003, and a version of the concluding section of Chapter 4 appeared in *Cambridge Literary Review* in October 2009. However, as I make clear in the main text, the chapters in Part Two of this book have mostly been published in earlier form. Chapter 6 first appeared in the *Times Higher Education Supplement* in February 1989 (and was re-printed in my *English Pasts*). The first three sections of Chapter 7 were given as talks on BBC Radio 3 in April 2000 and have not previously been published; one paragraph from the fourth section appeared in *English Pasts*, and the concluding paragraphs of that section appeared in *CAM: Cambridge Alumni Magazine* in 2006. A version of Chapter 8 originally appeared in the *London Review of Books* in December 2003 (and was reprinted in my *Common Reading*). Chapter 9 was published in the *Times Literary Supplement* in November 2009. The greater part of Chapter 10 appeared in the *London Review of Books* in November 2010; the final section appeared in *Guardian Online* in December 2010. I am grateful to the editors of these periodicals for permission to re-use this material here.

Index

PENGUIN POLITICS

THE IDEA OF JUSTICE
AMARTYA SEN

'The most important contribution to the subject since John Rawls' *A Theory of Justice*' Hilary Putnam, Professor Emeritus in Philosophy, Harvard University

Is justice an ideal, forever beyond our grasp? Or is it something that may actually guide our practical decisions and enhance our lives? In this major work, the Nobel Prize-winning economist and philosopher Amartya Sen presents a new approach to this question, arguing that mainstream theories of justice have so far, despite their many specific achievements, taken us in the wrong direction.

Public reason, Sen insists, plays a significant role in establishing what can make societies less unjust. But there are always choices to be made between alternative assessments of what is reasonable, and competing positions can each be well-defended. Rather than rejecting these pluralities, we should use them to construct a theory of justice that can accommodate divergent points of view.

'If a public intellectual is defined by his or her capacity to bridge the worlds of pure ideas and most far-reaching policies, Sen has few rivals'
David Aaronovitch, *The Times*

'A cornucopia of commonsense humane advice combined with analytical insight'
Samuel Brittan, *Financial Times*

'Elegant, literate, and reflective essays by an original thinker and a master of English prose' Jonathan Sumption, *Spectator*

PENGUIN ECONOMICS

WHOOPS! WHY EVERYONE OWES EVERYONE AND NO ONE CAN PAY

JOHN LANCHESTER

We are, to use a technical economic term, screwed. The cowboy capitalists had a party with everyone's money and now we're all paying for it. What went wrong? And will we learn our lesson – or just carry on as before, like celebrating surviving a heart attack with a packet of Rothmans?

If you want to know, but are the sort of person who finds it hard to tell the difference between a CDO, a CDS, an MBS and a toasted cheese sandwich, John Lanchester has mastered the finer points of finance so you don't have to. In *Whoops!* he explains, in language everyone can understand, what really happened – and what on earth we do next.

'This is what George Bernard Shaw might have called An Intelligent Person's Guide to the Crisis of Modern Capitalism, and everyone ought to read it' *Robert Harris, Sunday Times*

'The route map to the crazed world of contemporary finance we have all been waiting for. John Lanchester's superb book is everything its subject - the 2008 crash - was not: namely lucid, beautifully contrived, comprehensible to the reader with no specialist knowledge - and most of all devastatingly funny' *Will Self*

'Original…beautifully written…both entertaining and profoundly anger-inducing' *Chris Blackhurst, Evening Standard*

PENGUIN POLITICS

BLACK MASS
JOHN GRAY

From the bestselling author of *Straw Dogs*

Our conventional view of history and human progress is wrong. It is founded on a pernicious myth of an achievable utopia that in the last century alone caused the murder of tens of millions. In *Black Mass* John Gray tears down the religious, political and secular beliefs that we insist are fundamental to the human project and shows us how a misplaced faith in our ability to improve the world has actually made it far worse.

'The closest thing we have to a window-smashing French intellectual' Andrew Marr

'Causes vertigo when it does not cause outrage' *Sunday Times*

'Brilliant, frightening, devastating' John Banville, *Guardian*

'Savage. Gray raises profound and valid doubts about the conventional "plot" of modern history' *Financial Times*

PENGUIN PHILOSOPHY

GRAY'S ANATOMY: SELECTED WRITINGS
JOHN GRAY

'If humans are different from other animals it is chiefly in being governed by myths, which are not creations of the will but creatures of the imagination.'

'No traditional myth is as untruthful as the modern myth of progress. All prevailing philosophies embody the fiction that human life can be altered at will. Better aim for the impossible, they say, than submit to fate. Invariably, the result is a cult of human self-assertion that soon ends in farce.'

Why is progress a pernicious myth? Why do beliefs that humanity can be improved end in farce or horror? Is atheism a hangover from Christian faith?

John Gray, one of the most iconoclastic thinkers of our time, smashes through civilization's long cherished beliefs, overturning our view of the world and our place in it.

'The most prescient of British public intellectuals' Pankaj Mishra, *Financial Times*

'The most important living philosopher' Will Self

PENGUIN HISTORY

A HISTORY OF HISTORIES
JOHN BURROW

This unprecedented book, by one of Britain's leading intellectual historians, describes the intellectual impact that the study of the past has had in the western world over the past 2,500 years. It brings to life the work of historians from the Greeks to the present, including Livy, Tacitus, Bede, Froissart, Clarendon, Gibbon, Macaulay, Michelet, Prescott and Parkman, explaining their distinctive qualities and allowing the modern reader to appreciate and enjoy them. It sets out to be not the history of an academic discipline, but a history of choice: the choice of pasts, and the ways they have been demarcated, investigated, presented and even sometimes learned from as they have changed according to political, religious, cultural and patriotic circumstances.

Burrow argues that looking at the history of history is one of the most interesting ways we can try to understand the past. Nothing on the scale of or with the ambition of his book has yet been attempted in English.

'A triumphant success. The result is a highly enjoyable book, based on a vast amount of reading, written with attractive simplicity, brimming with acute observations, and often very witty. Anyone who wants to know what historical writing has contributed to our culture should start here' Keith Thomas, *Guardian*

'This book is magnificent: a daunting combination of vast range, profound learning and high literary art. In 500 superbly crafted pages (miraculously succinct for the task in hand), Burrow's chapters treat almost every important historian of the last two-and-a-half thousand years' John Adamson, *Sunday Telegraph*

PENGUIN HISTORY

HOMO BRITANNICUS
CHRIS STRINGER

Homo Britannicus tells the epic history of life in Britain, from man's very first footsteps to the present day.

Drawing on all the latest evidence and techniques of investigation, Chris Stringer describes times when Britain was so tropical that man lived alongside hippos and sabre tooth tiger, times so cold we shared this land with reindeer and mammoth, and times colder still when we were forced to flee altogether.

This is the first time we have known the full extent of this history: the Ancient human Occupation of Britain project, led by Chris, has made discoveries that have stunned the world, pushing back the earliest date of arrival to 700,000 years ago. Our ancestors have been fighting a dramatic battle for survival here ever since.

'This is a beautiful book on a fascinating subject, written by the world authority. What more could one ask?' Richard Dawkins

'A superlative achievement. *Homo Britannicus* is pure stimulation from beginning to end' Bill Bryson

'This book will be essential reading for all those interested in human history - or, indeed, in the story of the British landscape' Richard Fortey

PENGUIN CLASSICS

A TREATISE OF HUMAN NATURE
DAVID HUME

'Human Nature is the only science of man; and yet has hitherto been the most neglected'

One of the most significant works of Western philosophy, Hume's Treatise was published in 1739–40, before he was thirty years old. A pinnacle of English empiricism, it is a comprehensive attempt to apply scientific methods of obser-vation to a study of human nature, and a vigorous attack upon the principles of traditional metaphysical thought.

With masterly eloquence, Hume denies the immortality of the soul and the reality of space, considers the manner in which we form concepts of identity, cause and effect and speculates upon the nature of freedom, virtue and emo-tion. Opposed both to metaphysics and to rationalism, Hume's philosophy of informed scepticism sees man not as a religious creation, nor as a machine, but as a creature dominated by sentiment, passion and appetite.

This is the only unabridged edition of Hume's classic philosophy text, edited by Ernest C. Mossner. His introduction explains Hume's thought, and places it in the context of its times.

Edited and with an introduction by Ernest C. Mossner

'No man has justified the history of philosophy to a deeper or more disturbing degree' Isaiah Berlin

---

PENGUIN CLASSICS

THE SOCIAL CONTRACT
JEAN-JACQUES ROUSSEAU

'Man was born free, and he is everywhere in chains'

These are the famous opening words of a treatise that has not ceased to stir vigorous debate since its first publication in 1762. Rejecting the view that anyone has a natural right to wield authority over others, Rousseau argues instead for a pact, or 'social contract', that should exist between all the citizens of a state and that should be the source of sovereign power. From this fundamental premise, he goes on to consider issues of liberty and law, freedom and justice, arriving at a view of society that has seemed to some a blueprint for totalitarianism, and to others a declaration of democratic principles.

Translated and with an introduction by Maurice Cranston

He just wanted a decent book to read ...

Not too much to ask, is it? It was in 1935 when Allen Lane, Managing Director of Bodley Head Publishers, stood on a platform at Exeter railway station looking for something good to read on his journey back to London. His choice was limited to popular magazines and poor-quality paperbacks – the same choice faced every day by the vast majority of readers, few of whom could afford hardbacks. Lane's disappointment and subsequent anger at the range of books generally available led him to found a company – and change the world.

'We believed in the existence in this country of a vast reading public for intelligent books at a low price, and staked everything on it'
Sir Allen Lane, 1902–1970, founder of Penguin Books

The quality paperback had arrived – and not just in bookshops. Lane was adamant that his Penguins should appear in chain stores and tobacconists, and should cost no more than a packet of cigarettes.

Reading habits (and cigarette prices) have changed since 1935, but Penguin still believes in publishing the best books for everybody to enjoy. We still believe that good design costs no more than bad design, and we still believe that quality books published passionately and responsibly make the world a better place.

So wherever you see the little bird – whether it's on a piece of prize-winning literary fiction or a celebrity autobiography, political tour de force or historical masterpiece, a serial-killer thriller, reference book, world classic or a piece of pure escapism – you can bet that it represents the very best that the genre has to offer.

Whatever you like to read – trust Penguin.